Privacy

T0172446

Privacy: Algorithms and Society focuses on encryption technologies and privacy debates in journalistic crypto-cultures, countersurveillance technologies, digital advertising, and cellular location data.

Important questions are raised such as: How much information will we be allowed to keep private through the use of encryption on our computational devices? What rights do we have to secure and personalized channels of communication, and how should those be balanced by the state's interests in maintaining order and degrading the capacity of criminals and rival state actors to organize through data channels? What new regimes may be required for states to conduct digital searches, and how does encryption act as countersurveillance? How have key debates relied on racialized social constructions in their discourse? What transformations in journalistic media and practices have occurred with the development of encryption tools? How are the digital footprints of consumers tracked and targeted?

Scholars and students from many backgrounds as well as policy makers, journalists, and the general reading public will find a multidisciplinary approach to questions of privacy and encryption encompassing research from Communication, Sociology, Critical Data Studies, and Advertising and Public Relations.

Michael Filimowicz is Senior Lecturer in the School of Interactive Arts and Technology (SIAT) at Simon Fraser University. He has a background in computer-mediated communications, audiovisual production, new media art, and creative writing. His research develops new multimodal display technologies and forms, exploring novel form factors across different application contexts including gaming, immersive exhibitions, and simulations.

Algorithms and Society

Series Editor:
Dr Michael Filimowicz *is Senior Lecturer in the School of Interactive Arts and Technology (SIAT) at Simon Fraser University.*

As algorithms and data flows increasingly penetrate every aspect of our lives, it is imperative to develop sufficient theoretical lenses and design approaches to humanize our informatic devices and environments. At stake are the human dimensions of society which stand to lose ground to calculative efficiencies and performance, whether at the service of government, capital, criminal networks, or even a general mob concatenated in social media. At stake are the human dimensions of society which stand to lose ground to calculative efficiencies and performance, whether at the service of government, capital, criminal networks, or even a general mob concatenated in social media.

Algorithms and Society is a new series which takes a broad view of the information age. Each volume focuses on an important thematic area, from new fields such as software studies and critical code studies to more established areas of inquiry such as philosophy of technology and science and technology studies. This series aims to stay abreast of new areas of controversy and social issues as they emerge with the development of new technologies.

If you wish to submit a book proposal for the series, please contact Dr Michael Filimowicz michael_f@sfu.ca or Emily Briggs emily.briggs@tandf.co.uk

Digital Totalitarianism
Algorithms and Society
Edited by Michael Filimowicz

Systemic Bias
Algorithms and Society
Edited by Michael Filimowicz

Privacy
Algorithms and Society
Edited by Michael Filimowicz

Democratic Frontiers
Algorithms and Society
Edited by Michael Filimowicz

Deep Fakes
Algorithms and Society
Edited by Michael Filimowicz

For more information on the series, visit: https://www.routledge.com/Algorithms-and-Society/book-series/ALGRAS

Privacy
Algorithms and Society

Edited by
Michael Filimowicz

Routledge
Taylor & Francis Group

LONDON AND NEW YORK

First published 2022
by Routledge
4 Park Square, Milton Park, Abingdon, Oxon OX14 4RN

and by Routledge
605 Third Avenue, New York, NY 10158

Routledge is an imprint of the Taylor & Francis Group, an informa business

© 2022 selection and editorial matter, Michael Filimowicz; individual chapters, the contributors

The right of Michael Filimowicz to be identified as the author of the editorial material, and of the authors for their individual chapters, has been asserted in accordance with sections 77 and 78 of the Copyright, Designs and Patents Act 1988.

British Library Cataloguing-in-Publication Data
A catalogue record for this book is available from the British Library

Library of Congress Cataloging-in-Publication Data
Names: Filimowicz, Michael, editor.
Title: Privacy / edited by Michael Filimowicz.
Other titles: Privacy (Routledge (Firm) : 2022)
Description: Milton Park, Abingdon, Oxon ; New York, NY : Routledge, 2022. | Series: Algorithms and society | Includes bibliographical references and index.
Identifiers: LCCN 2021053462 (print) | LCCN 2021053463 (ebook) | ISBN 9781032002514 (hardback) | ISBN 9781032002545 (paperback) | ISBN 9781003173335 (ebook)
Subjects: LCSH: Data privacy. | Personal information management. | Cyber intelligence (Computer security) | Information technology—Social aspects.
Classification: LCC HD30.3815 .P75 2022 (print) | LCC HD30.3815 (ebook) | DDC 323.44/8—dc23/eng/20220107
LC record available at https://lccn.loc.gov/2021053462
LC ebook record available at https://lccn.loc.gov/2021053463

ISBN: 978-1-032-00251-4 (hbk)
ISBN: 978-1-032-00254-5 (pbk)
ISBN: 978-1-003-17333-5 (ebk)

DOI: 10.4324/9781003173335

Typeset in Times New Roman
by codeMantra

Contents

Illustrations

Figures

Table

Contributors

Sezgin Ateş (PhD) is a research assistant in the Department of Advertising and Public Relations at the Faculty of Communication Sciences, Anadolu University. His research focuses on consumer psychology, political consumption, communication studies, and political communication.

Dr. Tommy Cooke is a fellow at the Surveillance Studies Centre and professor of Sociology at Queen's University. He is principal investigator of A Day in the Life of Metadata, a multidisciplinary collaboration between social scientists, computer scientists, and humanities scholars to empirically demystify how governments and corporations harvest location metadata in smartphones in real time.

Naim Çınar is an assistant professor in the Department of Advertising and Public Relations at the Faculty of Communication Sciences, Anadolu University. He also has professional experience as a graphic designer in the advertising industry. His research interests include emerging technology and consumer trends, user-generated content, user data privacy, and digital methods in communication research. For more information, please visit his personal academic website: www.naimcinar.com.

Luke Heemsbergen (PhD) lights fires and builds bridges between digital communication and political life, where novel media make new relations and power structures visible and knowable. His work draws from Communications and Science and Technology Studies to create social focus on diverse technological subjects (e.g. WikiLeaks, 3D printing, Augmented Reality) and has engaged diverse national and international partners. His academic appointments have included time at Deakin University, The University of Melbourne, and Harvard's Berkman-Klein Centre, while he's worked in the private and public sectors, including serving in the Government of Canada's Department of Global Affairs.

Alexia Maddox (PhD) is a sociologist of technology and specializes in research engagement with communities, digital research methods, and socio-technical transformations. Her research focuses on the cultures in emerging digital frontiers, including crypto-based technologies such as cryptocurrencies and blockchain technologies, and digital pleasures such as digital drugs and ASMR. She is a Research Fellow at the RMIT Blockchain Innovation Hub, RMIT University.

S.L. Revoy is an independent scholar whose work intersects cultural studies, philosophy, media studies, and science and technology studies. They are particularly concerned with questions regarding the intersectional construction of subjectivity and in approaching problems related to these questions through the lenses of discourse analysis, critical theory, and intellectual history.

Karina Rider is a postdoctoral researcher with the Social Media Collective at Microsoft Research New England. Her research explores the dynamics and consequences of political action targeting digital technologies and the Big Tech industry. She received her PhD in Sociology from Queen's University.

Series Preface

Algorithms and Society

Michael Filimowicz

This series is less about what algorithms are and more about how they act in the world through "eventful" (Bucher, 2018, p.48) forms of "automated decision making" (Noble, 2018, loc. 141) in which computational models are "based on choices made by fallible human beings" (O'Neil, 2016, loc. 126):

> Decisions that used to be based on human reflection are now made automatically. Software encodes thousands of rules and instructions computed in a fraction of a second.
>
> (Pasquale, 2015, loc. 189)

> If, in the industrial era, the promise of automation was to displace manual labor, in the information age it is to pre-empt agency, spontaneity, and risk: to map out possible futures before they happen so objectionable ones can be foreclosed and desirable ones selected.
>
> (Andrejevic, 2020, p. 8)

> [M]achine learning algorithms that anticipate our future propensities are seriously threatening the chances that we have to make possible alternative political futures.
>
> (Amoore, 2020, p. xi)

Algorithms, definable pragmatically as "a method for solving a problem" (Finn, 2017, loc. 408), "leap from one field to the next" (O'Neil, loc. 525). They are "*hyperobjects*: things with such broad temporal and spatial reach that they exceed the phenomenological horizon of human subjects" (Hong, 2020, p. 30). While in the main the technological systems taken up as volume topics are design solutions to problems for which there are commercial markets, organized communities, or claims of state interest, their power and ubiquity generate new problems for inquiry. The series will do its part to track this domain fluidity across its volumes and contest, through critique and investigation, their "logic of secrecy" (Pasquale, 2015, loc. 68), and "obfuscation" (loc. 144). These new *social* (rather than strictly computational) problems that are generated can, in turn, be taken up by many critical, policy, and speculative discourses. At their most productive, such debates can potentially alter the ethical, legal, and even imaginative parameters of the environments in which the algorithms of our information architectures and infrastructures operate, as algorithmic implementations often reflect a "desire for epistemic purity, of knowledge stripped of uncertainty and human guesswork" (Hong, 2020, p.20). The series aims to foster a general intervention in the conversation around these often "black boxed" technologies and track their pervasive effects in society:

> Contemporary algorithms are not so much transgressing settled societal norms as establishing new patterns of good and bad, new thresholds of normality and abnormality, against which actions are calibrated.
>
> (Amoore, 2020, p.5)

Less "hot button" algorithmic topics are also of interest to the series, such as their use in the civil sphere by citizen scientists, activists, and hobbyists, where there is usually not as much discursive attention. Beyond private, state, and civil interests, the increasingly sophisticated technology-based activities of criminals, whether amateur or highly organized, deserve broader attention as now everyone must defend their digital identities. The information systems of companies and states conduct a general form of "ambient surveillance" (Pasquale, loc. 310), and anyone can be a target of a hacking operation.

Algorithms and Society thus aims to be an interdisciplinary series which is open to researchers from a broad range of academic backgrounds. While each volume has its defined scope, chapter contributions may come from many areas such as sociology, communications, critical legal studies, criminology, digital humanities, economics, computer science, geography, computational media and design, philosophy of technology, and anthropology, along with others. Algorithms are "shaping the conditions of everyday life" (Bucher, 2018, p. 158) and operate "at the intersection of computational space, cultural systems, and human cognition" (Finn, 2017, loc. 160), so the multidisciplinary terrain is vast indeed.

Since the series is based on the shorter Routledge Focus format, it can be nimble and responsive to emerging areas of debate in fast-changing technological domains and their sociocultural impacts.

References

Amoore, L. (2020). *Cloud Ethics: Algorithms and the Attributes of Ourselves and Others*. Durham: Duke University Press.

Andrejevic, M. (2020). *Automated Media*. New York: Taylor & Francis.

Bucher, T. (2018). *If...Then: Algorithmic Power and Politics*. Oxford: Oxford University Press.

Finn, E. (2017). *What Algorithms Want: Imagination in the Age of Computing*. MIT Press. Kindle version.

Hong, S-H. (2020). *Technologies of Speculation: The Limits of Knowledge in a Data-Driven Society*. New York: New York University Press.

Noble, S. U. (2018). *Algorithms of Oppression*. New York: New York University Press. Kindle version.

O'Neil, C. (2016). *Weapons of Math Destruction*. Broadway Books. Kindle version.

Pasquale, F. (2015). *The Black Box Society*. Cambridge: Harvard University Press. Kindle version.

Volume introduction

Michael Filimowicz

This volume on Privacy presents multidisciplinary discussions and case studies of key issues related to the transformations of practice, regulatory gaps, and social impacts of encryption and surveillance technologies.

Chapter 1 – "Distributing Journalism: Digital Disclosure, Secrecy, and Crypto-Cultures" by Luke Heemsbergen and Alexia Maddox – begins the volume by charting developments in distributed and crypto-journalism in connection to the cypherpunks movement and the rise to prominence of WikiLeaks. This sets the stage for an in-depth analysis of how coverage of the Capital riots on January 6, 2021, reflects key changes in journalistic public information-making practices.

Chapter 2 – "Centering Race in Analyses and Practices of Countersurveillance Advocacy: Mythologies of the Racialized Other in the Crypto Wars" by Karina Rider and S.L. Revoy – expands the discussion around encryption as a general technical solution for achieving effective countersurveillance to include racial constructions. Through discourse analysis on 16 years of US congressional hearings, they highlight the racial mythologization of criminals and how this has shaped public policy.

Chapter 3 – "Data Privacy in Digital Advertising: Towards a Post Third-Party Cookie Era" by Naim Çınar and Sezgin Ateş – analyzes the methods by which consumer behaviors are tracked online for the delivery of personalized advertising and have their personal data commodified in the marketplace. The technologies employed inevitably leading to privacy violations and regulations often do not keep up with the fast pace of these technical developments which allow for evermore effective web tracking and surveillance.

Chapter 4 – "Smartphones, APIs & GNSS (Not GPS) Location Data" by Tommy Cooke – provides a granular analysis of the specific algorithmic protocols and systems that track our location and movements via cellular technologies. These challenge our conception of privacy since much is mystified under the general heading of "GPS" and these increasingly precise tools make our location information available to firms around the world.

Acknowledgment

The chapter summaries here have in places drawn from the authors' chapter abstracts, the full versions of which can be found in Routledge's online reference for the volume.

1 Distributing Journalism
Digital Disclosure, Secrecy, and Crypto-Cultures

Luke Heemsbergen and Alexia Maddox

Introduction

This chapter engages with documenting how digital secrets and distributed disclosures are evolving cultures of journalistic and civic practice. The rise and shifts of new forms of distributing journalism trace a movement from private disclosures and exclusive stories to distributed disclosures and public made stories. Often, large datasets and diverse actors factor into the creation of such news stories. These shifts have occurred across techno-cultural contexts of openness and secrecy that have intertwined to redefine the work and identity of journalists.

The practice and promise of journalism in the western world has worn thin. Rosen (1999) suggests that a frame of competent professional bystander who reports on the events of public interest that roll by had fallen out of grace long before algorithmic steering and audience microcasting redefined news.

Foreseeing fractured and fractious publics, Rosen (1999, p. 19) offers journalism's purpose "not just to inform a public that may or may not emerge, but to improve the chances that it will emerge". That is to say that the press shapes everyday politics. It does so through the manufacture of stories: from how and who gathers facts, what they decide is news, and then how stories are presented and to whom. At the same time, markets for news and practices of journalism to fill them have suffered from radical external shifts of environment that are well known. Summarizing some of these shifts at the cusp of Social Media ubiquity, Carvajal, García-Avilés, and González (2012) offer that:

> As the advertising market disappears into a fragmented world of digital outlets and readers consume news for free, there is little if any money available to subsidise quality journalism. A lack of resources undermines reporting quality and fact-checking practices.

DOI: 10.4324/9781003173335-1

Bureau cuts, fewer news correspondents and the abuse of information received from agencies are simply a few consequences of this situation (Brogan, 2010; Starr, 2009). The one thing that can be capitalised is the demand for news products that continue to remain scarce, such as investigative reporting.

(Carvajal et al., 2012, p. 639)

Here, the need for new models for journalism, especially investigative journalism, echoes trends of media ecosystems shifting from centralized to distributed networks. In the broadcast model of centralized news production and consumption, insiders share secrets with other insiders who happen to be journalists. These journalist-gatekeepers then broadcast the stories they decide to make with the information they have. This process describes a classical "leaked" government communiqué being ready for the evening news. It does not, however, *explain* the democratic merit of centralized, gatekeeping news media. On the opposite end of the spectrum is a distributed model, where secrets first become available to the many – those people formerly known as the audience – who then make multiple stories and in doing so enact a new form of publicness. These renditions of what news is – across extremes of centralized and distributed models – are simplistic. Nevertheless, it serves to show the differences in specific models of journalism practice vis-à-vis the public: consider how Daniel Ellsberg carefully leaked documents to noted reporters, while WikiLeaks offered up literal wiki functionality to masses of data and humans. Stories could be created from and for audiences wide and far.

But WikiLeaks' wiki did not last. Wikileaks.org's distinct phases created permutations and combinations of journalism practice that drew light not only to new ways of making news, but the evolutionary complexity of claiming to be a force of transparency and truth in a data-rich world (Heemsbergen, 2021). Part of the complexity had to do with how these cultures attached to cryptography. The cypherpunks – a like-minded, liberty-focused group of computer scientists, coders, and civil libertarians, willed WikiLeaks into existence – rubbed up against structural powers of the state (Follis & Fish, 2020) and the market (Cammaerts, 2013). Paradoxically, part of the new digital machines that "killed secrets" (Greenberg, 2012) was a suite of cryptographic technologies that enabled the many to share data and communicate with each other in private or anonymously. This afforded new ways to organize secrets that in turn created new public information. The ethos that drove these cryptographic practices was not always aligned with traditional journalistic practice or ethics, or the traditional power differentials between western states and their journalists. We turn now from our brief introduction of journalism distributed to focus on cryptographic cultures themselves.

Note that as this chapter unpacks the ethos in distributed journalism, we highlight a set of techno-cultural practices that were not apparent or were potentially unprofessional in the earlier iterations of what was dubbed network journalism. We break from a *networked journalism* that acknowledges multi-platform, multi-voice, always on digital content machines (Beckett & Mansell, 2008) that is understood through a frame of convergence culture. Closer is how Van Der Haak, Parks, and Castells (2012, p. 2927) describe a "diffused capacity to record information, share it, and distribute it" that includes as novel digital tools crowdsourcing, data analytics, and automated writing tools, among other digital capacities offered to the journalist subject.

Yet even further, we suggest that cryptography brings a new suite of affordances to journalism that is worth identifying and exploring in technical and cultural affect. Here we align to Costa (2018) and Heemsbergen (2019) and suggest that rather than focus on cryptography's specific technical architectures, it is useful to focus on cryptographic practices of use within situated environments, namely how cultures of cryptography pervade and interface with journalism practice. How do cryptographic affordances in practice facilitate a model of distributed journalism? In summary, the early promise of networked journalism

Advertisement

READ THE
DOCUMENTS
Full PDF □

It cites a combination of recently obtained, still-unpublished data from outbreak investigations and outside studies showing that vaccinated individuals infected with delta may be able to transmit the virus as easily as those who are

Figure 1.1 Washington Post website.

gave way to a cacophony of feedback loops and even disinformation that were afforded by the corporate interests of Web 2.0 products focusing attention on the most divisive content (Ribeiro et al., 2019) to drive engagement. Some of what is left of the original networked journalism promise remains at the margins, present in a set of techno-cultural cypherpunk practices that open new ways of seeking, protecting, and then widely sharing what makes news, news. We are interested in showing how far the liminal and periphery of journalistic practice around cryptography has come. Note that we signal distributing journalism as a practice and action rather than a noun or standard of "distributed journalism". Its essence is tactical pushes into new distributions of making secret information public and then crafting public information. Cryptography helps with the former, and cryptographic cultures with the latter.

Strictly speaking, cryptography is the use and study of techniques to secure communications from being read by third parties or the public. In the digital age, these techniques form a ubiquitous layer of invisible digital infrastructures that enable and secure everything from banking online to watching DVDs and streaming Netflix. Yet as Bruun, Andersen, and Mannov (2020, p. 13) point out, employing cryptographic security systems "into the telecommunication data of millions of people reveal that data infrastructures and cryptographic systems are not just technical but also social and political forms". It is not just certain products and their corporate interests that are protected by cryptography, but our capacity to communicate as we intend in a digital world. Cryptography is utilized to *retain* the levels of privacy and security present in the analogue world (Narayanan, 2013) by offering a technical solution to the expectation of a whispered conversation, sealed envelope, or locked box. However, cryptography constitutes a method of rearranging power in ways that were previously unavailable. These new power relations have confused states, offered moral panics for law enforcement, and in their ideal deployment enabled a utopian zero-trust society tied to libertarian ideologies. As Bauman et al. (2014) have it, there is a tension between the concerns raised in public debates about data security and the promises of emerging cryptographic protocols. Similarly, Bruun et al. (2020, p. 13) observe that in political speeches and public debates, citizens' trust that governments and tech companies will protect their data is framed as important and essential. In the environments of emerging cryptographic technologies, such as blockchains, bitcoin, and multiparty computation (MPC), a promise to provide "trustless trust" and abandon the need for trusted intermediaries, authorities, and institutions is articulated (Bruun et al., 2020). In the next section, we more fully explore these ideologies and cultures to frame how they might relate to the cryptographic distribution of journalism.

Crypto-cultures and the public interest

How such techniques and cultures of cryptography distribute journalism's practice and worth is a question of public interest. Follis and Fish (2020) argue that contradictory relationships emerge through the entanglements of hacking, journalism, the state, and political action that we discuss in this chapter. We contend that these relationships are not always contradictory and at times represent a convergence of politics within and across institutions, services, and people that bridge between the technopolitics of cypherpunks and journalism. This section will introduce the cultural milieu surrounding cryptography, present a typology of crypto-cultures, and then signpost the merger of these practices and politics with journalism. Moving through the realism of the scientific journalism spruiked by WikiLeaks founder Julian Assange, this section will lead us into the more diverse realm of crypto-journalism.

Turning for a moment to the history of technical cryptography is useful to describe the conditions created by cryptographic cultures and the cypherpunk moment. Before the 1970s, governments, particularly that of the US, stifled public pursuits in crypto (Levy, 2001). However, under pressure from industry and various organizations, in 1973 the US Government instigated work toward the Data Encryption Standard. In 1975, a proposal put forward by IBM was accepted and a modified version was adopted as the Federal Information Processing Standard 46 (FIPS-46) in 1977 and renamed the US Federal Data Encryption Standard (DES)[1] (Dooley, 2018, p. 169). The DES became the most widely used computer encryption algorithm of the twentieth century, to be replaced more recently with the Advanced Encryption Standard (AES) in 2001 (Dooley, 2018, p. 167). During the same time period as the development of the DES, the first publicly available work on public-key cryptography was published, "New Directions in Cryptography" (Diffie & Hellman, 1976), which presented a cryptographic solution to the key exchange problem faced by most major businesses, government offices, and academic institutions using computers and computer networks (Churchhouse, 2002).

These events created the conditions for the cryptographic movement that coalesced through the cypherpunks in the early 1990s. They became a:

> semi-organized group at a casual 1992 meeting of about 20 computer scientists, coders, and civil libertarians in San Francisco led by Hughes, Intel employee Tim May, and computer scientist John Gilmore, all three young retirees thanks to their early career successes.

In late 1992, Eric Hughes, Timothy C May, and John Gilmore founded a small group that met monthly at Gilmore's company Cygnus Solutions in the San Francisco Bay Area. The group convened to discuss the big problems in programming and cryptography (Jansen, 2018). The name cypherpunk was coined by Jude Mihon in 1995 and is a portmanteau of cipher (cypher) and punk, which was thought by the group to be an excellent marketing approach (Bartlett, 2015). From the Cyphernomicon (May, 1993), May provides the frequently asked question (FAQ) response as to the origin of the group's name:

"2.4.10. "Where did the name 'Cypherpunks' come from?"
+ Jude Milhon, aka St. Jude, then an editor at "Mondo 2000," was at the earliest meetings...she quipped "You guys are just a bunch of cypherpunks." The name was adopted immediately.
- The 'cyberpunk' genre of science fiction often deals with issues of cyberspace and computer security ("ice"), so the link is natural. A point of confusion is that cyberpunks are popularly thought of as, well, as "punks, " while many Cyberpunks are frequently libertarians and anarchists of various stripes. In my view, the two are not in conflict.
- Some, however, would prefer a more staid name. The U.K. branch calls itself the "U.K. Crypto Privacy Association." <check this> [sic] However, the advantages of the name are clear. For one thing, many people are bored by staid names. For another, it gets us noticed by journalists and others.
-
- We are actually not very "punkish" at all. About as punkish as most of our cyberpunk cousins are, which is to say, not very." (May, 1993)

Usefully, this explainer untangles cypherpunk from the cyberpunk genre of fiction made popular by sci-fi writers such as William Gibson. Featherstone and Burrows (1995, p. 3) define the cyberpunk fiction genre as engaging with "visions of the future worlds of cyberspaces, with all their vast range of technological developments and power struggles". While there are, of course, continued overlaps in the utopian/dystopian vision that accompanies cryptographic practices, we will continue to refer to cypherpunks in order to orient the cultural context on cryptographic practice.

The group expanded its reach through the cypherpunks mailing list of like-minded, liberty-focused individuals who used then-new pretty good privacy (PGP) encryption to keep their messages private (Jansen, 2018), and just a few months later, Eric Hughes published "A Cypherpunk's Manifesto". In her historical contextualization of the rise of Bitcoin, a cryptocurrency, Swartz (2018) observes that the founders of the cypherpunks email list defined privacy as "the power to selectively reveal oneself to the world", and points out that privacy was positioned as both defensive and informational privacy and as a natural right which authorities could not bestow. Thus to protect privacy, they saw the need to produce cryptographic information systems outside of the purview of government or corporate entities (Bartlett, 2015). The rights to political life needed to be more evenly distributed.

This value parallels the role of journalism as independent of but relational to the nation-state in democratic systems (i.e. fourth estate). However, as Narayanan (2013) points out, for cypherpunks, crypto was at the core of a vision of how technology would cause sweeping social and political change, weakening the power of governments and established institutions. He points to the technical roots of crypto in the work of David Chaum (1985), whose article entitled "Security without Identification: Transaction Systems to Make Big Brother Obsolete" is telling. This is, perhaps, where there is divergence between the value field of public interest journalism and cryptography. While journalism within a democratic system aims ideally to be independent of government (i.e. not a voice piece of state propaganda), it does not aim to undermine it per se but to make information public through "truth telling". In the section below, we see how WikiLeaks broke this mold.

Drawing from Swartz's analysis we observe that the design of information protocols, as the design of the larger social contract, intersects with public interest journalism to make information public *and* make public information. This intersection is expressed through the way cryptographic technologies enable and constrain the basis of communicative shared reality. However, this process is also intended to be transformative. Swartz points to how Hughes's (1993) manifesto emphasized that "people must come and together deploy these systems for the common good", to develop and use shared communication systems that would form the basis of a new society predicated on privacy. It is at this point that we can also observe that cryptographic technologies seek to transform communicative infrastructures into public-making processes.

Providing a useful discussion of the role of technology in augmenting public discourse and diversification of voices that could enter it, Follis and Fish (2020) argue that initially the technology gave individuals and activists the capacity to act with impact on a global scale for criminal or disruptive purposes, but also for traditionally liberal purposes such as dissent, transparency, protest and to spur political change or democratic debate. As an example, they argue that the pro-democracy leaks of Snowden, Manning, and Ellsberg, alongside the weaponized data dumps and doxxing campaigns of Anonymous, LulzSec, and Phineas Fisher, demonstrate how different methodologies of scale and time affect networked public spheres and media ecologies to provide differential opportunities for debate, dissent, resistance and, increasingly, state disruption.

Through her historical research, Swartz presents the political make-up of the cypherpunk email list in the words of its cofounder Tim May. In the elist "FAQs" called the Cyphernomicon, he described its members as a mix of "radical libertarians, some anarcho-capitalists, and even a few socialists". Additionally, in a post to the mailing list in 1993, he suggests that not all cypherpunks are anarcho-capitalist libertarians and indicates that "many are just interested in privacy, others want to see power taken away from multinational corporations, and so on". As Narayanan (2013) suggests, there was an (anarcho-) political to pragmatist spectrum amongst crypto-cultures:

> I don't mean to suggest that this belief was mainstream in the crypto or tech communities—when Cypherpunk cofounder Tim May handed out copies of his *Crypto Anarchist Manifesto* at the 1988 Crypto conference in Santa Barbara, the academics "pretty much ignored him." But the cypherpunks were vocal enough and persuasive enough that *Wired*, for example, was a prominent early champion of the movement.
>
> (Narayanan, 2013, p. 76)

In considering the cypherpunk cultural origins, Swartz observes, and what is evident in the typology we discuss, that while it is difficult to draw clear boundaries around the subjectivities present, it is analytically useful to attempt to do so. For example, a commonly associated but not homologous term with the cypherpunk movement is crypto-anarchism (Narayanan, 2013). Narayanan (2013, p. 76) succinctly articulates how this political philosophy, in its idealized form, recognizes no laws except those that can be described by math and enforced by code. We see this particular aspect commonly traversing into hacker, blockchain/cryptocurrency, and Open Source Software (OSS) cultures in the "code as law" refrain.

A (Working) typology of crypto-cultures

In order to clarify the relationships, value overlaps and disjuncture of cryptographic actors with journalistic practice, we present a (working) typology of relevant crypto-cultures. In developing a typology of crypto-cultures, we seek to articulate an array of formal and informal actors from computer-savvy armchair adventurers, activists (hacktivists), and journalists to commercial and state actors who are involved in deploying encryption technologies and the hacker toolkit for, and at times against, the public or civic interest. Situating these crypto-cultures in the context of the cypherpunks privileges the place of digital cryptography – a central technology of whistleblower platforms such as WikiLeaks – in their technological worldview (Anderson, 2021). This typology will set the scene for the range of actors that coalesce around crypto-journalism discussed later in this section. The subsequent sections will then discuss cryptography and its cultures in journalism and those hacking subsets of cypherpunks spilling over into doxxing and being institutionalized within journalism mastheads. Within these discussions, you will see the cast of actors, discussed below, take the stage.

The discussion thus far has highlighted that those engaged in cryptography range from anarcho-libertarians to crypto-pragmatists and that they hold a variety of standpoints toward the use of cryptography and its role in the public interest. Within the emergence of crypto-cultures, scientists, activists, and hackers have populated our accounts. These form your archetypal actors within the crypto-space. For the hacker, their toolkit includes penetration "testing" of encrypted environments, sometimes with the aim of creating potential data leaks, or the insertion of ransomware, sometimes with the aim of creating data hostages. This toolkit universally consists of the application of tools and resources to target various aspects of computer infrastructure – applications, networks, systems, hardware, and software as well as people (Martin, 2017). This is where crypto-for-security knowledge enters. What differentiates an ethical hacker (white hat) from an ambivalent (grey hat) or malicious actor (black hat), for example, is not the tools they use but their motivation, legality, permission, and pre-knowledge of others regarding their actions (Martin, 2017).

In terms of crypto-activists, we have the existing notion of the hacktivist (a portmanteau of hacker and activist). George and Leidner (2019) observe that hacktivists work toward the ultimate aim of using the hacker toolkit to achieve social action or political objectives. They define hacktivism as a subset of digital activism and a form of direct action which is enacted through computer code that exposes information, destroys data, or disrupts operations. Additionally, they highlight the murky and slippery nature of categorizing hacktivism as in the public interest by classifying actions into three categories: cyberterrorism, civic hacking, and patriotic hacking. We will meet the patriotic hacker in the final section of this chapter. As Heemsbergen (2021) points out in his discussion of Anonymous, not all direct action has notable political effects. The hacktivist cohort is perhaps the closest to the Cypherpunks. However, closer still are those who advocate the use of privacy technologies such as Tor, PGP encryption, cryptocurrencies, and blockchain technologies to usher in a new communicative reality.

While the crypto-cohort may or may not identify as hacktivists, many amongst them could be considered crypto-activists who engage in direct action through the application of encryption technologies to construct new communicative realties (Maddox et al., 2016). An example of a crypto-pragmatist involved in direct action can be found in the work of Phetsouvanh et al. (2021), who are less concerned with why and more concerned with how, demonstrating the centering of cryptography in direct action. In this article, the author presents mechanisms to strengthen whistleblowing platforms designed for journalistic purposes. The rationale for doing so is presented as "Whistleblowing is a crucial enabler of checks and balances needed to make a system, be it an organization, or a country operate in an accountable manner" (Phetsouvanh et al., 2021, p. 438). The author, in essence, presents the design of a larger social contract of privacy, security, and the accountability of an amorphous other. The "mechanisms" contain within them coded parameters that enable the ability to make information public *and* make public information.

In an adjunct but overlapping activity space, we identify commercial interests in cryptography. As evident in the Californian ideology that formed a cultural foundation for Silicon Valley giants such as Google and Apple, these commercial interests arose through "a loose alliance of writers, hackers, capitalists, and artists from the West Coast of the United States [who] have succeeded in defining a heterogeneous orthodoxy for the coming information age" (Barbrook & Cameron, 1996). Steve Jobs hacked payphones to not pay long distance charges. This ideology can still be seen threading through the way Apple and Google vied with each other over consumer trust and the privacy principle through offering end-to-end encryption of communications and encrypted cloud storage in their products in 2014 (Lever, 2014). These practices resulted in a standoff between Apple and the Federal Bureau of Investigation (FBI) and saw the reemergence of "the cryptowars" or cypher wars around customer privacy (Barrett, 2016).

These wars surfaced in the early 1990s when Phil Zimmerman sent his new PGP public-key encryption software to a couple of friends who uploaded the program to the Internet in 1991 (Levy, 1994). PGP is an encryption system that lets people communicate privately online. It supports encrypting, decrypting, and authenticating digital files and online communication. At the time, the US government had identified that public availability of strong cryptography must be curtailed, which Zimmerman speculates was because the government knew what a pivotal role cryptography was destined to play in the power relationship with its people (Zimmerman, 1991). Zimmerman decided to publish PGP electronically for free that year in response to the proposed Senate Bill 266, a 1991 omnibus anticrime bill which outlined amongst other things that:

> providers of electronic communications services and manufacturers of electronic communications service equipment shall ensure that communications systems permit the government to obtain the plain text contents of voice, data, and other communications when appropriately authorized by law.
>
> (Zimmerman, 1991)

In PGP's documentation, Zimmermann called his program "guerrilla freeware"; however, the patented algorithms Zimmerman incorporated had already been licensed to RSA Data Security Inc., which had no intention of letting Zimmermann corrode its markets (Levy, 1994). In 1993, he faced three years of legal battle on the technicalities that the US considered the "export" of cryptographic hardware and software to first require a munitions license for export and second to utilize a weaker encryption approach (shorter key) before being exported (Dooley, 2018, p. 232). The court case was dropped when they realized it was time to relax these laws and that PGP encryption was now widely distributed and out of their control (Dooley, 2018). After more time wrangling with RSA's president Jim Bidzos and working with the Massachusetts Institute of Technology (MIT) professors who originally owned the patent, a version of PGP (2.6) was released that circumvented the patent infringement issues.

In 1999, the Clinton administration threw out the export control regime in its closing months; however, the desire by governments to have access to private communications through a backdoor or "trapdoor" constantly resurfaces. Advances in cryptography and the shifting value fields in the sector see particular exceptions emerge, for example, with regards to detecting images of child sexual abuse (Leswing, 2021). Apple has reported it will employ a single purpose system, Child Sexual Abuse Material (CSAM), to detect images from the cloud uploaded photo libraries of its customers using a process called hashing, where images are transformed into unique numbers that correspond to that image. The proposed scan process, which is facing fierce backlash from outside researchers, academics, and the information security community, instigates when the image upload is instigated on the phone and prior to the image being added to the cloud library (Cox, 2021). Focusing on the customer privacy aspect, Apple argues that its system is more private for users than previous approaches to eliminating illegal images of child pornography, because it uses sophisticated cryptography on both Apple's servers and user devices. The debates surrounding Apple agreeing to report child exploitation images uploaded to iCloud to US law enforcement are reminiscent of the fear that one exception to customer privacy protection opens the possibility of its abuse by governments, such as profiling for photos of political protest.

Much further away from these jousts between regulatory authorities and the commercial application of personal encryption technologies, commercial interests surrounding encryption technologies also include largely unregulated organizations such as secretive spyware firms and online services for public disclosure for fraud and safety markets. Heemsbergen (2021) presents the ambivalent case of We-Leakinfo, which illustrates the murky territory of commercial practice. WeLeakinfo offered paying customers the chance to check if their passwords had been stolen by hackers by comparing logins to known hacked-and-posted databases. However, a joint law enforcement operation across Europe found that they were also selling actual stolen user accounts and passwords in bulk. More recently, this grey commercial zone is illustrated in the case of Pegasus spyware. Recently, military grade Pegasus spyware licensed by an Israeli firm to governments for tracking terrorists and criminals made the news when it was used against the company's terms and conditions in attempted and successful hacks of 37 smartphones belonging to journalists, human rights activists, and business executives (Priest et al., 2021). The resulting Pegasus Project, a media consortium response along with Amnesty's Security Lab, examined these violations, making publicly visible the function and capacities of these products through the application of the hacker toolkit. These events, the cryptowars, the unregulated public disclosure market, and the Pegasus Project, illustrate how commercial actors, states, hackers, and journalists are embroiled in a murky typology of crypto-cultures. Furthering the murk, Follis and Fish in their book *Hacker States* (2020) move states from the regulatory and policing position toward cryptographic technologies to active protagonists in their deployment and penetration. They observe that for states, the deployment of the hacker toolkit is about combining surveillance with hacking repositories of data and code that will serve as the basis for new political technologies and pressure points (Follis & Fish, 2020).

A (working) synthesis of the crypto-cultures typology is as follows; however, as the above discussion highlights, these distinctions are by nature murky, slippery, and secretive. Within the canon of crypto-actors, we have malicious actors involved in the penetration of encrypted environments for the purposes of data capture and hostage taking through ransomware. These actors are motivated by money and notoriety. Utilizing the same hacker toolkit, we have hacktivists and crypto-activists, who range from privacy advocates, through armchair adventurers, and to software creators. Whistleblowing platforms, PGP encryption, and Tor are some of their many contributions. These actors are motivated by goals most similar to the early cypherpunks. We also have commercial actors whose services incorporate privacy technologies for consumers but range to security and statecraft espionage technologies. Primary motivations are both financial and ideological, with weak regard for the regulatory and policing functions of the state. State actors become complicit through their deployment of crypto-technologies, the hacker toolkit, and at times the recruitment of notorious hackers as political technologies for statecraft. Within this typological quagmire, a new communicative reality emerges within which the journalist must conduct investigative reporting for the public interest. The investigative journalist merges the hacking toolkit and encryption technologies with digital storytelling and secure communications. This leads us from the typology of actors within crypto-cultures to the specific practices of crypto-journalism.

Crypto-journalism

While the diversity within our crypto-cultures typology is important to recognize, it is nevertheless the purpose of this chapter to focus on the parts of these crypto-technical practices that relate to shifts in journalistic practice and leverage the crypto-cultural ethos to make public information. Within our analysis, we observe an interrelated yet distinct set of practices that signal the transformation of communicative practices and with this, the shift in power configurations of who can do what, from what. It is within this context that we argue for an emergence of crypto-journalism.

To set the context for this, we follow Follis and Fish (2020) in veering away from the language of information warfare or technological "arms race" to describe the deployment of encryption technologies alongside the hacker toolkit for the securitization, dissemination, and breaching of information and communication infrastructures. They argue for the need to retain a focus on how this transitional moment heralds increases in surveillance, intrusions, exfiltrations, hacked elections, and social media leaks ahead of us. Follis and Fish present the notion of high breach societies to emphasize the need for the development of mechanisms for algorithmic justice that govern human and nonhuman actions. While we agree with this noble goal, we look instead to the mundane practices and transformations to journalism that come with this socio-technical shift. In doing so, we argue that the data deluge, consisting of leaks and dumps of secrets, make possible distributed journalistic practices. The convergence of cryptography with public interest journalism moves a step beyond making information public to making public information.

To zero in on the site of transformation within public interest journalism, the making public of secrets, the relations between whistleblowers and journalism in the digital age now depends on encrypted communications to keep "anonymous sources" anonymous. Yet, more than those mechanics, Di Salvo suggests professional journalism now reflects an ongoing "mixture of hacking and reporting" (Anderson, 2021, p. 174) that creates new types of story making and new ways to read those stories:

> Whistleblowing platforms are also a visible example of "boundary-work" happening at the interconnection between the journalistic and the hacking fields, and offer visible evidence of how journalism itself is increasingly accepting stances that are coming from outside its own boundaries and that are shaping its current culture, tools and technologies.
> (Di Salvo & Leaks, 2020, p. 175)

When we consider the cultural milieu and shifts in power configurations of who can do what, and from what, that ties together with big data, we start to see the emergence of crypto-journalistic practice. This is not algorithmic journalism or big data journalism, but an assemblage with specific socio-technical cultures that are articulated within the typology of crypto-cultures. Crypto-journalism is meant to reference the "punk" in cypherpunk. In the next section, we discuss examples of crypto-journalism at work to interrogate what making public information looks like and what type of public is afforded through these practices.

Torrents of leaks and distributing data journalism: *leaking, mining, stealing, maintaining*

Here, we cover some of the patterns and cases that make up crypto-journalistic practices as they've evolved since WikiLeaks. This section introduces distributed journalist practices that spread leaked secrets to the many; leverage public "big data" and analytics to "mine" insights that would have otherwise remained secret; consider how hacked data transfigures journalism practice; and finally reflect on how these practices are maintained. These practices of *leaking, mining, stealing, and maintaining* public secrets is not a complete account, but does offer insight to the creation of public secrets in distributed journalism. The section that follows explication of these themes details an in-depth case study of how these practices evolved into proto-institutionalized practice by 2021, but this section sets the techno-cultural stage for that intervention by tracing the practices that influenced the institutionalization of distributed journalism.

Even before WikiLeaks, Cryptome.org was a site where purloined documents could be distributed to the many through the internet. It once even made news by hosting the content of a secret WikiLeaks email distribution list, as WikiLeaks experienced its first growing pains (Cryptome, 2006). The point here though is that Cryptome and then WikiLeaks offered up the secrets of others to the networked public, so that sense could be made of them by whoever looked. That is to say that while an elite cadre in the newsroom once made visible and then made sense of news "stories" and the evidence that backed them up, these practices were distributed to a wider net by sites like WikiLeaks.

The interesting techno-cryptographic aspects of WikiLeaks practices were twofold. First, WikiLeaks' sources were encouraged to project themselves and their material by using Tor and other cryptographic technologies to share material with WikiLeaks. These technologies provided anonymity to who was sending what, while also protecting the documents and data from third parties while in transit. Second and less reported was the strange paradox in how Assange claimed to use cryptographic infrastructure itself to siphon secrets into public view. Specifically, instead of relying on whistleblowers to offer leaks in the public interest, Assange claimed to have control of a Tor exit node where encrypted documents in transit on the Tor network became unencrypted and decipherable. While WikiLeaks could not see who sent documents to whom, the documents were made readable. By 2007, Assange is reported to have stated in relation to the Tor network that:

> Hackers monitor chinese [sic] and other intel as they burrow into their targets, when they pull, so do we....Near 100,000 documents/emails a day. We're going to crack the world open and let it flower into something new....We don't even know a tenth of what we have or who it belongs to.
>
> (Assange in Young 2010)

These uses of crypto-cultures and cryptographic technologies to arrive at news shows praxis of cracking open a model of distributing what could become news as well as the sources that such stories were sourced from. The stories from secrets were coming from distributed sources using cryptographic technologies – whether the sources knew they were contributing or not. In this model, secrets leaked to widespread interpretation from those around the world.

The crypto-cultural aspects of WikiLeaks' vanguard of crypto-journalism were put into a blazing light of publicity via Julian Assange's experiments to bring about a journalistic philosophy that he calls "scientific journalism". As Assange (2010) explains:

> We work with other media outlets to bring people the news, but also to prove it is true. Scientific journalism allows you to read a news story, then to click online to see the original document it is based on. That way you can judge for yourself: Is the story true? Did the journalist report it accurately?
>
> (Assange, 2010)

There are two things of note here. First is a move to trustless intermediaries. The views of the newsman or the prominence of the source of the "scoop" no longer matter. As Saroj Giri (2010, p. npn) notes, WikiLeaks "challenged power by challenging the normal channels of challenging power". At the same time, what is important here is provenance of the documents insofar the trustless anonymity of transmission and the public intermediaries that govern their spread are of secondary importance. The objects of news are the organizations suffering their secrets leaked; the subject of public information the secrets make public are not even the secrets themselves, but the organization that hid them.

Second is the question of what type of information is now public and made into news. For Assange, the information worth sharing were those secrets that linked together "conspiracies" of knowledge that hitherto skirted public detection, interpretation, and action. In a more cynical framing, Zizek (2011) commented that the information WikiLeaks was making into public information wasn't the truth itself (everybody knows the deals were rotten; that's how it goes), but that WikiLeaks made the lies that hid secrets undeniable. WikiLeaks exposed the necessary lies of society in ways that falsified governing ideologies that were holding up hierarchical social power relations. The realpolitik of the world was undeniable, un-cyphered, and reportable in a way that urged a new publicness to emerge.

An alternative model of distributed journalism that is less dependent on torrenting secrets is enabled when public data is scraped into secret insights. The secrets here are such not from being actively hidden from view, but by needing to be *mined* from the latent background noise of datafied everyday life. The International Consortium of Investigative Journalists (ICIJ) proves a good example of explaining the differences. The ICIJ has procured, distributed, and analyzed a series of "leaks" to make news. These include Offshore Leaks (2013) through to the more well-known Panama Papers (2016) and Paradise Papers (2017). However, by 2018, they had uploaded a database called "The Implant Files" that was different. Instead of relying on leaked databases from whistleblowers, intelligence agencies, or otherwise, the ICIJ decided to create its own database by compiling publicly available information about medical device safety from various jurisdictions around the world. In their words:

> To increase transparency, we are sharing a publicly searchable database of more than 70,000 recalls and safety warnings in 11 countries...The Implant Files is the story of the pain behind the gain of devices rushed to market, aggressively sold, then implanted in people.
>
> (Shiel, 2018)

While it might be easy to interpret this as big data journalism (see Lewis, 2015) at work, it is important to show how the shift for the ICIJ's practice retained key aspects of distributing journalism. The ICIJ kept its distributed infrastructures (from people to technologies) that craft news stories from disparate data but no longer relied on leakers to provide its data cum secrets. Here the secrets were hiding in plain view. The ICIJ's cross-jurisdictional network was required to make sense of and bring attention to the implications of these data. Built from being dropped secrets, this distributed infrastructure was able to pursue new goals and data gathering techniques.

Next, we consider attack-based "leaking" where actors break into organizations, pilfer their secrets, and make them publicly accessible. Most notoriously here is Anonymous, a loose collective of actors that ran various political actions intertwined with digital crypto-cultures (Coleman, 2014). Specifically, we can look here to the campaigns of AnonLeaks, which saw itself as "remarkable advance of WikiLeaks.... [where] Anonymous-type hacks simply steal and torrent the family jewels of the spies, officials, lobbyists and corporations believing they own the territory in order to show the extent of their secret predations on the public" (Anonymous, 2011). AnonLeaks spurred a new entity called Potentially Alarming Research: Anonymous Intelligence Agency (Par:AnoIA) that frequently published hack-based disclosures. Material released on Par-AnoIA.net by early 2013 included government documents from Azerbaijan, Cambodia, China, Italy, South Africa, and Queensland (Australia), documents from the German Chamber of Commerce, Organisation for Security and Cooperation in Europe, and Italian State Police. Of note is that this material is no longer online.

The final model of distributing journalism discussed here, past *leaking* secrets to the many, *mining* secrets from a public multitude of data, and *stealing* secrets by any means, responds to the fact that all these newsworthy secrets must remain accessible to be public information. There is a need to *maintain* public secrets. Most famously, Edward Snowden's archive of documents was hosted – privately it should be pointed out – at The Intercept, before the database was shut down to "focus on other editorial priorities", according to Bruder and Maharidge (in Heemsbergen, 2021, p. 125). Past latent.torrent files distributed among anonymous systems, a new form of public secret maintainer is evolving. New entrants into this space such as Distributed Denial of Secrets (DDoS) are open to host myriads of "private databases" of newsworthy content on their domain. More than opening a few torrents of individual databases, DDoS seeks to institutionalize the archiving and categorizing of those elements of distributing journalism that allow its continued existence: the data itself, gathered from various projects around the web as resource. The services side of distributed crypto-cultures is not new, however, being pioneered by Aaron Swartz and Kevin Poulsen to provide a secure and anonymous uploading and storing of data as a plug-and-play solution for news organizations. Their work on "Strong box" morphed into the more widely known "SecureDrop" service, which is in use by many media outlets worldwide (Di Salvo, 2021). These types of services continue to evolve with reference to the crypto-cultures that work for and against them: with designs to mitigate the impact of denial of service attacks (Phetsouvanh et al., 2021) and tools for rapid archiving (Fiorella et al., 2021), for instance. Other modes of maintaining to consider include projects like the Zuckerberg Files. Rather than unearth Facebook secrets (see the *Wall Street Journal*'s "The Facebook Files"), this project seeks to ensure a digital archive of "all public utterances of Facebook's founder and CEO" are available for critique and insight into how Zuckerberg "conceives of his own company's role in the policy and ethical debates surrounding social networking" due to its unique position around sharing and information privacy (2021).

These various models (leaking, mining, stealing, maintaining) show a varied evolutionary trajectory of how journalism is being redistributed as it encounters the cypherpunk cultures that enjoy distributed logics of governance and practice to solve problems, create community, and affect change. As we think about the varied evolutionary path of such practices, it is interesting to turn our attention to in-depth analysis of one recent case study that shows just how far crypto-cultures and distributed logics of control now enmesh in journalistic practice. As such, the next section turns to the recording and analyzing the events of 6 January 2021 at the US capitol.

The public accounting of the capitol riots: a case of crypto-journalism and hyperreal disclosure

The spotlight of publicity shone from *The New York Times* in 2021 points to the URL slug https://www.nytimes.com/spotlight/us-capitol-riots-investigations.[2] There, disparate sources, databases, and journalistic talents come together to make public information. Included in the assortment of data are scraped (read hacked) videos from the Parler, video feeds from competitor media (Fox News), and other pictures that are designed to identify the movement and identities of those who marched on and stormed the capitol. *The New York Times* used hacked videos, social media posts, and CCTV footage to not only make marchers visible, but name them as individuals. Within the crypto world, this is referred to as doxxing.

The New York Times

VISUAL INVESTIGATIONS

Tracking the Oath Keepers Who Attacked the Capitol

By Stella Cooper, Ben Decker, Anjali Singhvi and Christiaan Triebert   Jan. 29, 2021

Alleged conspirators

Jessica Watkins   Donovan Crowl

Other raid participants

Figure 1.2 The New York Times reporting on the January 6 rioters.

At play is an institutional acceptance of how crypto-cultures work and what they offer to making public information. One might comment that news' focus on real-time coverage shifted here to hypertime, where the methods of recombinant reporting make public information not in real time, but through hypertime afforded by backtracing the Global Positioning System (GPS) movement, parallel video feeds, and saved social media posts, in order to form new stories for public consumption. These temporal hyperlinks – worked out before and after the event – between varied texts, timelines, and platforms created new information from which new news could be created. There is also a sense of hyperreal disclosure through distribution. Reporting practice is not carried out by professionals watching events march by, but by recombining and reorganizing the hyper-distributed sets of information that have *been made* public and then recrafting these into public information. How hyper-distributed information (hacked, encrypted,

Inside the Capitol

All 10 Oath Keepers we tracked can be seen inside the building in and around the Rotunda, along with Ms. Watkins and Mr. Crowl, who are in the selfie video below on the left. In the clip on the right, three of the 10 members are seen praying.

Figure 1.3 The New York Times reporting using datascraping.

delivered for amplification) informs public information presents a new case of making news. Real-time news cycles might make way to hyper-distributed ones.

Below, we detail the mediated narrative of 6 July at the capitol, to document how hyper-distributed information required crypto-enhanced practices and technologies deployed to make newsworthy events. During the Trump administration, the hyper-partisan times and accompanying proliferation of fake news were both globally newsworthy and rampantly evident on social media. Fact checking and counter-truth claims heralded the emergence of a "misinformation beat" within the practice of investigative journalism (Haughey et al., 2020). It also further supported the rise of crowdsourcery, in which journalists adapt in the context of crisis events to serve the public interest by stitching social media information together for their readers (Dailey & Starbird, 2014). Trump, a populist leader, utilized social media to build constituencies and wield power (Tollefson, 2021), particularly through the playground of misinformation, disinformation, and conspiracy. One such purveyor of conspiracy was QAnon, the followers of which he retweeted (Tollefson, 2021). As his presidency came to an end, Trump pushed the idea that the election would be illegitimate when he suggested that postal ballots can be falsified. QAnon had merged with the anti-vaccine movement and embraced the theory that the 2020 US presidential election was rigged. This group then started to promote the "storming" of the capitol through social media (Argentino, 2021):

> Things came to a head at a 6 January rally, when Trump told attendees, 'If you don't fight like hell, you're not going to have a country anymore.' He then called for them to march to the US Capitol, just as Congress was preparing to certify Democrat Joe Biden as the next US president.
>
> (Tollefson, 2021)

The call results in the "March to save America" (Van Dijcke & Wright, 2021). As we are about to observe, from the ground up, this riot has been described and narrated in new, crypto-enhanced formats and in hyperreal time in which the technologies and hacktivist practices deployed make newsworthy events. An early taste from the scientific grey literature gives us a sense of the methodologies of news-making to come:

> This study combines granular location data from more than 40 million mobile devices with novel measures of community-level voting patterns, the location of organized hate groups, *and the entire georeferenced digital archive of the social media platform Parler.*
>
> (Van Dijcke & Wright, 2021, emphasis added)

This is not, initially, publicly available data that reveals open secrets from existing social media and other data sets through their automated aggregation, relational interlacing, and contextual synthesis. This is leaked data, gained through the hacker toolkit for nationalistic hacktivist purposes and honed by pseudonymous actors to make public information that forms in hyperreal time to make news events and doxx geo-targeted actors. The final section will delve deeply into this event to provide a case study for the inversion of crypto-journalism, where stories are stitched together by digital vigilantes (Favarel-Garrigues et al., 2020) from hacked social media data sets to enact a retributive justice through doxxing. Beyond crowdsourc(er)ing stories via social media and citizen journalism sits the realm of digital vigilantism, which during the capitol riots became institutionalized within journalism mastheads.

But first, what happened to provoke this direct digital action for justice and retribution?

> By 6 January, the repressive forces, paramilitaries, white supremacist members of police forces, and military branches assembled as a counter-mob, a vigilante posse to save the country from an imaginary theft. Murdering police, threatening to lynch elected officials, and screeching irrational creeds and conspiracy theories, this mob seized the capital with little resistance and official hesitation.
>
> (Rosati, 2021)

This human tragedy was also a tragedy of democracy and highly visible on social media, in more ways than one. During the January 6 assault on the Capitol Building in Washington, DC, rioters posted photographs and videos of their rampage on social media (Bushwick, 2021). Shortly after a pro-Trump mob stormed the Capitol, the FBI posted a tweet requesting any information that could help identify people who participated in the riot (Kelly, 2021). Local dating sites showed profiles of newcomers who said they planned to be in town for a few days and wanted to meet local people, making veiled references to protest activities, while others wore clothing or displayed other evidence of sympathy to President Donald Trump. Following the riots, dating app users used dating sites as a way to identify and report those who may have participated in the riot (West, 2021).

However, these crowdsourced doxxing practices did not stop with laborious individual account identification. The platforms participants used in the riot ranged from mainstream sites such as Facebook to niche ones such as Parler – a social networking service popular with right-wing groups (Bushwick, 2021). Hacktivists exploited a bug in Parler to download all of the right-wing social media platform's contents before Amazon Web Services stopped hosting the platform (Greenberg, 2021). The data that they obtained included pictures and videos which contained geolocation metadata revealing exactly how many of the site's users had taken part in the invasion of the US Capitol building. It also included thousands of images of unmasked faces, many of whom participated in the Capitol riot, although perhaps not all. As Gillespie (2021), quoting Bruns, points out, there is a possibility that someone might be identified for merely looking like another person or being an innocent bystander.

A website called Faces of the Riot appeared online, showing nothing but a grid of more than 6,000 images of faces, each one tagged only with a string of characters associated with the Parler video in which it appeared. In an interview with the site's creator, Greenberg (2021) reports that he used simple open source machine learning and facial recognition software to detect, extract, and deduplicate every face from the 827 videos that were posted to Parler from inside and outside the Capitol building on January 6. He reports the goal of Faces of the Riot is to allow anyone to easily sort through the faces pulled from those videos to identify someone they may know or recognize who took part in the mob or even to reference the collected faces against FBI wanted posters and send a tip to law enforcement if they spot someone.

The Parler archive has also been converted into an interactive map of the Capitol building attack, combining GPS metadata and the videos uploaded by Parler users. It was playfully subtitled "Y'all Qaeda" at the time of posting by its anonymous developer using the pseudonym Patr10tic. It offers a recombination of facts and cultures that produces hyper-news-making processes, called upon by various actors – traditional or otherwise. In his article, Campbell (2021) argues that the map and other like projects may prove vital to investigating how the events of January 6 took place. Vigilantes with handles like "deep state dogs" and hashtag communities of #seditionhunters remain active into 2021.

These acts of the naming and shaming people involved in the capitol riot through hacked and recompiled social media data sets to support their reporting to law enforcement could be considered an extension of digital vigilantism practices (Dunsby & Howes, 2019) and a form of nationalistic hacktivism. Making public information was achieved through the public-making processes of direct action associated with cryptographic cultures and the hacker toolkit. Crypto-actors are threaded throughout these events in order to make public information from a desire for retributive justice in defense of the US democratic institution and processes. In doing so, they have prompted a new model for investigative journalism, which leverages both cultures and technologies that were once at the margin of journalistic practice – both in terms of identity and ethos. This surprising institutional vanguard for new models of distributive investigative news-making creates a new alignment of cypherpunk influence toward public information.

Conclusion

This chapter introduced shifting paths of disclosure and reportage that make public information. We hoped to show how WikiLeaks' cypherpunk influences have pervaded into sets of journalistic practice that continue to redistribute the making of public information. While tropes like "scientific journalism" and big data leaks offer new technical practices for journalists to consider in making stories, there is also a related set of cultural practices about who and what makes the news that are, in concert, distributing what journalism is. Past "networked journalism", there are political effects of distributing journalism that have come to appropriate some of the logics of crypto-cultures into public information-making practices. The various cultures that surround crypto actors – in reference to journalistic practice that we've identified – include malicious actors (data capture and cryptographic ransom), crypto-activists (pushing privacy further), and commercial actors (that accelerate and resist state control). These cultures come together through combinations of leaking, mining, stealing, and maintaining secrets in new ways to make the news. As our case study showed, these cultural practices are moving from the margin to institutional regimes of news production. This means *The New York Times* scraping videos from Parler to identify and then disclose via its own reporting the identities of public transgressors as a major investigative story. Such practices are not unfamiliar to hackers who've doxxed individuals to affect public, political, or private purposes. That news institutions perform the same set of actions to make this information public creates a new kind of public information and a new set of journalistic practices that are both decentralized and unregulated cyphers to the public good.

References

Anderson, P. D. (2021). Book Review: Digital Whistleblowing Platforms in Journalism: Encrypting Leaks. *New Media & Society, 23*(6), 1731–1734. doi:10.1177/14614448211000664

Anonymous. (2011). HBGary More Leaked Emails. Retrieved from http://thepiratebay.org/torrent/6172442

Argentino, M.-A. (2021). QAnon and the Storm of the U.S. Capitol: The Offline Effect of Online Conspiracy Theories. Retrieved from https://theconversation.com/qanon-and-the-storm-of-the-u-s-capitol-the-offline-effect-of-online-conspiracy-theories-152815

Assange, J. (2010). Don't Shoot Messenger for Revealing Uncomfortable Truths. Retrieved from https://www.theaustralian.com.au/in-depth/wikileaks/dont-shoot-messenger-for-revealing-uncomfortable-truths/news-story/43b912ca277c90355fab12cc83cd4e69

Barbrook, R., & Cameron, A. (1996). The Californian Ideology. *Science as Culture, 6*(1), 44–72. doi:10.1080/09505439609526455

Barrett, B. (2016). The Apple-FBI Battle Is Over, But the New Crypto Wars Have Just Begun. Retrieved from https://www.wired.com/2016/03/apple-fbi-battle-crypto-wars-just-begun/

Bartlett, J. (2015). Cypherpunks Write Code. Retrieved from https://www.americanscientist.org/article/cypherpunks-write-code

Bauman, Z., Bigo, D., Esteves, P., Guild, E., Jabri, V., Lyon, D., & Walker, R. B. J. (2014). After Snowden: Rethinking the Impact of Surveillance. *International Political Sociology, 8*(2), 121–144. doi:10.1111/ips.12048

Beckett, C., & Mansell, R. (2008). Crossing Boundaries: New Media and Networked Journalism. *Communication, Culture & Critique, 1*(1), 92–104. doi:10.1111/j.1753–9137.2007.00010.x

Bruun, M. H., Andersen, A. O., & Mannov, A. (2020). Infrastructures of Trust and Distrust: The Politics and Ethics of Emerging Cryptographic Technologies. *Anthropology Today, 36*(2), 13–17. doi:10.1111/1467–8322.12562

Bushwick, S. (2021). What the Capitol Riot Data Download Shows about Social Media Vulnerabilities. Retrieved from https://www.scientificamerican.com/article/what-the-capitol-riot-data-download-shows-about-social-media-vulnerabilities/

Cammaerts, B. (2013). Networked Resistance: The Case of WikiLeaks. *Journal of Computer-Mediated Communication, 18*(4), 420–436. doi:10.1111/jcc4.12024

Campbell, I. C. (2021). A Parler Archive is being Converted into an Interactive Map of the Capitol Building Attack. Retrieved from https://www.theverge.com/2021/1/14/22231749/parler-interactive-map-video-gps-capitol-attack

Carvajal, M., García-Avilés, J., & González, J. (2012). Crowdfunding and Non-Profit Media. *Journalism Practice, 6*(5/6), 638–647. doi:10.1080/17512786.2012.667267

Chaum, D. (1985). Security without Identification: Transaction Systems to Make Big Brother Obsolete. *Communications of the ACM, 28*(10), 1030–1044. doi:10.1145/4372.4373

Churchhouse, R. F. (2002). *Codes and Ciphers: Julius Caesar, the Enigma, and the Internet.* Cambridge: Cambridge University Press.

Coleman, E. G. (2014). *Hacker, Hoaxer, Whistleblower, Spy: The Many Faces of Anonymous.* London, New York: Verso.

Costa, E. (2018). Affordances-in-practice: An Ethnographic Critique of Social Media Logic and Context Collapse. *New Media and Society, 20*(10), 3641–3656. doi:10.1177/1461444818756290

Cox, J. (2021). Apple Delays Release of Child Abuse Scanning Tech after Backlash. Retrieved from https://www.vice.com/en/article/y3d9dj/apple-delays-release-of-child-abuse-scanning-tech-after-backlash

Cryptome. (2006). Email from WL to D. Ellsberg. Retrieved from http://cryptome.org/wikileaks/wikileaks-leak.htm

Dailey, D., & Starbird, K. (2014). Journalists as Crowdsourcers: Responding to Crisis by Reporting with a Crowd. *Computer Supported Cooperative Work, 23*(4–6), 445–481. doi:10.1007/s10606-014-9208-z

Di Salvo, P. (2021). Securing Whistleblowing in the Digital Age: SecureDrop and the Changing Journalistic Practices for Source Protection. *Digital Journalism, 9*(4), 443–460. doi:10.1080/21670811.2021.1889384

Di Salvo, P., & Leaks, E. (2020). *Digital Whistleblowing Platforms in Journalism*. Cham: Palgrave Macmillan.

Diffie, W., & Hellman, M. (1976). New Directions in Cryptography. *IEEE Transactions on Information Theory, 22*(6), 644–654. doi:10.1109/TIT.1976.1055638

Dooley, J. (2018). *History of Cryptography and Cryptanalysis: Codes, Ciphers, and their Algorithms*. Springer.

Dunsby, R. M., & Howes, L. M. (2019). The NEW Adventures of the Digital Vigilante! Facebook Users' Views on Online Naming and Shaming. *Australian & New Zealand Journal of Criminology, 52*(1), 41–59. doi:10.1177/0004865818778736

Favarel-Garrigues, G., Tanner, S., & Trottier, D. (2020). Introducing Digital Vigilantism. *Global Crime, 21*(3–4), 189–195. doi:10.1080/17440572.2020.1750789

Featherstone, M., & Burrows, R. (1995). *Cyberspace/Cyberbodies/Cyberpunk: Cultures of Technological Embodiment*. Sage.

Fiorella, G., Godart, C., & Waters, N. (2021). Digital Integrity: Exploring Digital Evidence Vulnerabilities and Mitigation Strategies for Open Source Researchers. *Journal of International Criminal Justice*. doi:10.1093/jicj/mqab022

Follis, L., & Fish, A. (2020). *Hacker States*. Cambridge, MA: MIT Press.

George, J. J., & Leidner, D. E. (2019). From Clicktivism to Hacktivism: Understanding Digital Activism. *Information and Organization, 29*(3), 100249. doi:10.1016/j.infoandorg.2019.04.001

Gillespie, E. (2021). FBI, Rioters and Social Media: The Pitfalls of Online Vigilantism. Retrieved from https://www.sbs.com.au/news/the-feed/fbi-rioters-and-social-media-the-pitfalls-of-online-vigilantism

Giri, S. (2010). WikiLeaks beyond WikiLeaks. Retrieved from https://www.metamute.org/en/articles/WikiLeaks_beyond_WikiLeaks

Greenberg, A. (2012). *This Machine Kills Secrets: How WikiLeakers, Hacktivists, and Cypherpunks Are Freeing the World's Information*. Random House.

Greenberg, A. (2021). This Site Published Every Face From Parler's Capitol Riot Videos. Retrieved from https://www.wired.com/story/faces-of-the-riot-capitol-insurrection-facial-recognition/

Haughey, M. M., Muralikumar, M. D., Wood, C. A., & Starbird, K. (2020). On the Misinformation Beat: Understanding the Work of Investigative Journalists Reporting on Problematic Information Online. *Proc. ACM Hum.-Comput. Interact., 4*(CSCW2), Article 133. doi:10.1145/3415204

Heemsbergen, L. (2019). Killing Secrets from Panama to Paradise: Understanding the ICIJ through Bifurcating Communicative and Political Affordances. *New Media and Society, 21*(3), 693–711. doi:10.1177/1461444818804847

Heemsbergen, L. (2021). *Radical Transparency and Digital Democracy: WikiLeaks and Beyond*. Bingley: Emerald Publishing.

Hughes, E. (1993). A Cypherpunk's Manifesto. *Crypto Anarchy, Cyberstates, and Pirate Utopias.*

Jansen, E. C. (2018, April 17). The Cypherpunk Movement and the Creation of Cryptocurrency. Retrieved from https://www.finivi.com/cypherpunk-and-the-creation-of-cryptocurrency/

Kelly, M. (2021). FBI Received over 100,000 Pieces of Digital Evidence after Capitol Attack. Retrieved from https://www.theverge.com/2021/1/12/22227633/doj-fbi-evidence-capitol-trump-riot-attack

Leswing, K. (2021). Apple Will Report Images of Child Sexual Abuse Detected on iCloud to Law Enforcement. Retrieved from https://www.cnbc.com/2021/08/05/apple-will-report-child-sexual-abuse-images-on-icloud-to-law.html

Lever, R. (2014). 'Crypto Wars 2.0' Have Begun After Privacy Moves By Apple And Google. Retrieved from https://www.businessinsider.com/afp-new-privacy-battle-looms-after-moves-by-apple-google-2014-9?r=AU&IR=T

Levy, S. (1994). Cypher Wars: Pretty Good Privacy Gets Pretty Legal. Retrieved from https://www.wired.com/1994/11/cypher-wars/

Levy, S. (2001). *Crypto: How the Code Rebels Beat the Government--Saving Privacy in the Digital Age.* New York: Penguin.

Lewis, Seth C. (2015). Journalism in an Era of Big Data. *Digital Journalism, 3*(3), 321–330. doi:10.1080/21670811.2014.976399

Maddox, A., Barratt, M. J., Lenton, S., & Allen, M. (2016). Constructive Activism in the Dark Web: Cryptomarkets and Illicit Drugs in the Digital 'Demimonde'. *Information Communication and Society, 19*(1), 111–126. doi: 10.1080/1369118X.2015.1093531

Martin, C. D. (2017). Taking the High Road: White Hat, black Hat: The Ethics of Cybersecurity. *ACM Inroads, 8*(1), 33–35. doi:10.1145/3043955

May, T. (1993). Cyphernomicon. Retrieved from https://nakamotoinstitute.org/static/docs/cyphernomicon.txt

Narayanan, A. (2013). What Happened to the Crypto Dream? Part 1. *IEEE Security & Privacy, 11*(2), 75–76. doi:10.1109/MSP.2013.45

Phetsouvanh, S., Datta, A., & Tiu, A. (2021). On unlinkability and Denial of Service Attacks Resilience of Whistleblower Platforms. *Future Generation Computer Systems, 118*, 438–452. doi:10.1016/j.future.2021.01.030

Priest, D., Timberg, C., & Mekhennet, S. (2021). Private Israeli Spyware Used to Hack Cellphones of Journalists, Activists Worldwide. Retrieved from https://www.washingtonpost.com/investigations/interactive/2021/nso-spyware-pegasus-cellphones/

Ribeiro, F. N., Saha, K., Babaei, M., Henrique, L., Messias, J., Benevenuto, F., … Redmiles, E. M. (2019). *On Microtargeting Socially Divisive Ads: A Case Study of Russia-linked ad Campaigns on Facebook.* Paper presented at the Conference on fairness, accountability, and transparency, Chicago.

Rosati, C. (2021). "Mob Rule in Shadow and Light". *Human Geography, 14*(1), 156–160. doi:10.1177/19427786211007593

Rosen, J. (1999). *What are Journalists For?* London: Yale University Press.

Shiel, F. (2018). About The Implant Files Investigation. Retrieved from https://www.icij.org/investigations/implant-files/about-the-implant-files-investigation/

Swartz, L. (2018). What was Bitcoin, What Will it Be? The Techno-economic Imaginaries of a New Money Technology. *Cultural Studies, 32*(4), 623–650.

Tollefson, J. (2021). Tracking QAnon: How Trump Turned Conspiracy-theory Research Upside Down. *Nature: International Weekly Journal of Science, 590*(7845), 192. doi:10.1038/d41586-021-00257-y

The Zuckerberg Files. (2021). Frequently Asked Questions. https://zuckerbergfiles.org/frequently-asked-questions/

Van Der Haak, B., Parks, M., & Castells, M. (2012). The Future of Journalism: Networked Journalism. *International Journal of Communication (Online)*, 2923. Retrieved from https://search.ebscohost.com/login.aspx?direct=true&db=edsglr&AN=edsglr.A317781187&authtype=sso&custid=deakin&site=eds-live&scope=site

Van Dijcke, D., & Wright, A. L. (2021). Profiling Insurrection: Characterizing Collective Action Using Mobile Device Data. *Available at SSRN 3776854*. doi:10.2139/ssrn.3776854

West, D. M. (2021). Digital Fingerprints are Identifying Capitol Rioters. Retrieved from https://www.brookings.edu/blog/techtank/2021/01/19/digital-fingerprints-are-identifying-capitol-rioters/

Zimmerman, P. ([1991]1999). Why I Wrote PGP. Retrieved from https://www.philzimmermann.com/EN/essays/WhyIWrotePGP.html

Zizek, S. (2011). Good Manners in the Age of wikiLeaks. *London Review of Books, 33*(2), 9–10. Retrieved from http://www.lrb.co.uk/v33/n02/slavoj-zizek/good-manners-in-the-age-of-wikileaks

Notes

1 https://csrc.nist.gov/csrc/media/publications/fips/46/3/archive/1999-10-25/documents/fips46-3.pdf

2 https://www.nytimes.com/spotlight/us-capitol-riots-investigations

2 Centering Race in Analyses and Practices of Countersurveillance Advocacy

Mythologies of the Racialized Other in the Crypto Wars

Karina Rider and S.L. Revoy

Introduction

In 2016, Karina attended an international conference called RightsCon. The annual gathering brought together technologists, activists, scholars, and policy makers to discuss issues pertaining to digital technologies, human rights, and civil liberties. Just before lunch on the second day, Karina attended a panel titled "Witnessing Police Violence, On and Off the Internet," organized by Morgan Hargrave with WITNESS; Taina Angeli Vargas with the Ella Baker Center; and Malkia Devich-Cyril from the Center for Media Justice (now Media-Justice). The panelists addressed questions regarding activists' fight against state surveillance. How can activists—especially those fighting police brutality—defend themselves against surveillance when they are often unaware of the kinds of technologies that the state has at their disposal? Devich-Cyril had this to say about these questions:

> To some degree, I think that people know that they're being surveilled. We know that, right? Young people in particular are aware that they have to code their language and code their interactions online [...] And I don't mean code the way y'all mean code. And I don't mean encrypt the way y'all mean encrypt. But, like, how we protect and hide what we are talking about, and who we're talking to, and all those kinds of things. Can I just say, as an aside, I think that it's interesting that the encryption debate is so—it's so lodged within this wonky—if I might say—white, techy world, when in fact people of color been encrypting for generations, you know what I'm saying? People of color know all about encryption and how to code.

DOI: 10.4324/9781003173335-2

Although Devich-Cyril acknowledges that encryption can provide a layer of security for people of color at risk of violence and harassment—at one point arguing that Twitter needs to do more to ensure users' safety by encrypting direct messages on the platform—they also criticize the narrow, essentialist understanding of encryption which permeates tech circles. By characterizing debates about encryption as being "lodged" within a "white, techy world," Devich-Cyril draws attention to how many technologists have a limited understanding of the relationship between technology and social justice; in particular, they are unaware of (or downplay) how people of color have developed tactics over generations to protect themselves from violence and create safe spaces through analogical forms of encryption, such as coded speech. Instead, they conceptualize encryption as a circumscribed technolegal intervention detached from analyses of how surveillance is structured by racism and white supremacy.

Devich-Cyril's discussion provides a generative entry point for thinking through the ambivalence of encryption. On the one hand, encryption can be crucial in situations where activists—many of them people of color, queer, and/or undocumented—are at risk of violence from individuals, organized groups, and the state. On the other hand, as Devich-Cyril points out, activists and technologists can overestimate the power of encryption to ensure safety on its own; minimize the importance and sophistication of tactics people of color have developed over generations; and ignore how surveillance disproportionately targets people of color.

This chapter contributes to research on countersurveillance advocacy by troubling our assumptions about encryption's universal ability to protect vulnerable groups from state violence, while building on scholars' and activists' arguments that encryption debates frequently ignore questions of race. Rather than presuppose encryption as a countersurveillant, pro-privacy technology which can be implemented to protect groups from the state (what West [2021] calls determinist conceptualizations of encryption), we explore how encryption has served as a space for negotiating the competing logics of mass incarceration and neoliberal economic development—logics which are fundamentally structured by race. By examining popular, mythological conceptions underscoring encryption policy debates and reconsidering them as constitutive of a space of frequently racialized state violence, we aim to demonstrate to scholars and digital rights advocates the importance of centering race in countersurveillance advocacy and research. Doing so can trouble existing assumptions about encryption while generating new questions for future research.

Throughout this chapter, we present findings from a discourse analysis of federal encryption policy debates from 1990 to 2016. During this period, policy makers and members of the law enforcement and intelligence communities aggressively advocated for encryption regulation in the form of mandatory decryption capabilities; state actors set the terms of the debate as being not about whether the federal government *should* be able to demand decryption, but rather what the most efficient and palatable options were for designing such a capability: the state or private manufacturers. The most infamous of these proposals is the Clipper Chip, a cryptographic device to be embedded into telephones and other devices sold by American companies that would afford law enforcement the ability to decrypt communications. Companies and digital rights activists pushed back against these proposals, arguing that encryption should be deregulated—at the time, federal law prohibited US companies from exporting products with encryption—so that American companies could flourish in emerging global markets for information technology (IT) products and in the process protect user privacy through self-regulation. Our analysis demonstrates that these policy debates were fundamentally structured by mythological constructions of racialized others by (a) the state, which conjured myths of violent, sexual deviants to push for encryption regulation, and (b) the market, which drew upon nascent anxieties about foreign governments overpowering the US because of globalization. Eventually, the two sides came to a compromise: the Clinton administration dropped its proposals for mandatory decryption while lifting export controls, allowing US companies to sell their IT products abroad. At the same time, however, they organized informal backroom deals in which companies agreed to provide law enforcement with access to their customers' encrypted communications. This created a situation wherein racialized populations were caught in a discursive double-bind between the exclusionary demonizing practices inherent in myths used to justify encryption regulation (and, by extension, the carceral institutions bolstered by mandatory decryption) and resulting practices of predatory inclusion in which people of color are included in American companies' user bases and subjected to racialized surveillance as a result.

In the first section, we explore research on encryption as a tool for protecting privacy and countering surveillance, highlighting the different ways in which advocates and scholars have presented a narrow conceptualization of encryption which ignores questions of race. The following section presents the findings of our empirical investigation of federal policy debates over encryption from 1990 to 2016: first, how policy makers as well as police and intelligence officials habitually invoke mythological constructions of racialized criminal figures in order to advocate for encryption regulation and how corporations responded by stoking fears about a possible globalization not led by the US, but by foreign countries such as China, employing in their own way a different mythological figure of the threatening racial Other. The next section situates these findings in recent explorations of the co-construction of racial capitalism and network capitalism; here, we argue that deregulating encryption is a crucial step in setting the stage for future processes of predatory inclusion (Cottom, 2020). We conclude by emphasizing the importance of accounting for race when researching and advocating for technologies assumed to be universal countersurveillance tools. Despite the centrality of racialized mythological figures to encryption policy debates, digital rights advocates left the carceral and neoliberal logics untouched. This represents an opportunity moving forward; continuing encryption policy debates can provide technical experts, countersurveillance advocates, and scholars a space to contest ongoing racism in the US.

Encryption and countersurveillance advocacy

Without a doubt, encryption is a critical tool for vulnerable populations trying to protect themselves from violence and harassment, whether from organized groups, individuals, or governments. A 2015 report from David Kaye, the UN special rapporteur on freedom of expression, draws a direct link between encryption and freedom of expression, opinion, and the right to receive information and ideas. According to the report, encryption can "provide individuals and groups with a zone of privacy online to hold opinions and exercise freedom of expression without arbitrary and unlawful interference or attacks" (Kaye, 2015, p. 7). This is particularly important for civil society groups and individuals who are victims of "targeted surveillance, distributed denial of service attacks, and online and offline intimidation, criminalization and harassment [...] Encryption and anonymity enable individuals to avoid or mitigate such harassment" (Kaye, 2015, p. 8). Kaye's conceptualization draws from a "cryptographic imaginary" constructed by digital rights advocates that links encryption to democratic values by "establishing that encryption may be a precondition for democratic self-expression and association, by fostering zones of privacy where communities of individuals can join together without fear of surveillance" (West, 2018, p. 11). It follows then that in order to ensure civil society organizations and individuals have access to strong encryption, the IT firms which build, run, and service the majority of our communication channels need to be pressured into encrypting user data by default. Following the Snowden disclosures in 2013, many American companies—such as Apple and Google—faced mounting pressure from users and digital rights advocates to strengthen encryption in their products (McLaughlin, 2015).

However, focusing advocacy efforts on petitioning tech firms to change their products can legitimize corporations as protectors of the common good as well as the de facto providers of social services. In their study of submissions made to Parliament concerning the draft Investigatory Powers Bill in the UK, Stevens and Allen-Robertson (2021) found that civil liberties groups, digital rights organizations, and corporations tended to conflate encryption and human rights when opposing the bill. The problem with this conflation is that:

> the technology industry is thus utilising its privileged position as providers of encryption technologies to conflate their own activities with human rights protection, and to frame their data-driven activities of 'surveillance capitalism' [Zuboff, 2015] as innocuous and distant from state surveillance practices.
>
> (Stevens and Allen-Robertson, 2021, p. 2)

Similarly, Gürses et al. (2016, p. 586) note that despite the Snowden disclosures being "disastrous for the reputations of major tech corporations," they have been able to recuperate some of the damage because:

> the deployment encrypted services can now serve as the basis of public relations campaigns. The idea that solutions to societal problems can come from technical progress and sophistication in the private sector is the bread and butter of Silicon Valley corporations.

Framing the problem of government surveillance as something which can be addressed using corporate technologies means that advocates are inadvertently legitimizing tech firms as the natural providers of social goods.

In addition to positioning American tech firms as providers of social goods, scholars have argued that digital rights advocacy often provides a narrow understanding of encryption as an intervention into a technolegal problem, a tendency that has several consequences. First, there is evidence that the narrow framing of encryption as ipso facto a technolegal intervention against government overreach obstructs activists' ability to build broad coalitions across issue areas—particularly those concerned with racial inequality—which is only becoming more crucial as digital technologies saturate our institutions and everyday lives. In their interviews with a range of activists following the Snowden disclosures, Dencik et al. (2016) found little overlap between digital rights groups focused on technolegal interventions, including encryption, and other social justice organizations. Aouragh et al. (2015) similarly argue that the division of labor between activists and technical developers must be overcome to develop true alternatives to the commercial platforms the former frequently rely on for organizing.

Second, encryption advocacy frequently ignores the ways in which surveillance is fundamentally structured through intersecting lines of race, class, gender, ability, and nationality. For example, advocates often frame the problem of government surveillance as having to do with the scope of data collection; the problem, they argue, is that all individuals are under suspicion rather than the few who should be investigated (Gürses et al., 2016). This framing establishes a problematic demarcation between mass and targeted surveillance, with the latter being implicitly (or sometimes explicitly) held up as the desirable state of affairs. Therefore:

> these discussions fail to give space to those who are on the receiving end of global surveillance programs and linked forms of violence, such as extrajudicial killing, torture, and impoverishment including populations in the United States and Europe whose racialization has been integral to histories of colonialism, plantation slavery, and empire. (Gürses et al., 2016, p. 577).

In general, technolegal framings of interventions into surveillance tend to be depoliticizing. Although activists often face pressure to frame their arguments in terms their targets will find acceptable—for instance, by arguing to cash-strapped local governments that mass surveillance is expensive—to achieve their goals, doing so can also "[limit] our understanding of the implications of these data-driven practices that underpin contemporary surveillance and [dilute] their politicized nature" (Dencik et al., 2016, p. 8).

To remedy these shortcomings, scholars have proposed new frameworks which center analyses of racism and white supremacy. Rexhepi (2016, p. 2) argues that "to unsettle, decenter and rethink veillance theories beyond the taxonomies of surveillance inside liberal democracies, a critical intervention needs to destabilize and disrupt sur/

violence by shifting its focus from the center to the periphery." Simone Browne's work is a crucial step in this direction. Browne (2015) centers theorizing race and racism in thinking through the dynamics and consequences of both historical and contemporary surveillance. In doing so, Browne (2015, p. 8) develops the concept of *racializing surveillance*, in which "enactments of surveillance reify boundaries along racial lines, thereby reifying race, and where the outcome of this is often discriminatory and violent treatment." Racializing surveillance does not solely distribute harm along racial lines, but simultaneously shapes collective understandings of race.

Countersurveillance advocates also reproduce and reify understandings of race as they attempt to counteract state surveillance schemes. For instance, advocates frequently refer to George Orwell's *1984* as a quintessential example of the dystopian future we will inevitably realize if we allow the government to engage in mass surveillance (Gürses et al., 2016). The problem is that Orwell tacitly depicts mass surveillance as normalized where non-Western countries are concerned due to his use of totalizing mass surveillance as the novum of his dystopian UK; relying on this novel to understand the dynamics of mass surveillance "undermine[s] a political reading that would attend to the racial, gendered, classed, and colonial aspects of the surveillance programs" being critiqued (Gürses et al., 2016, p. 577). The use of such touchstones, centered as they are on the threat of figures of the Other and their oppressive, immoral practices as counter to the intrinsic values of Western states, should attune us to the broader use of such mythological tropes when considering the real policy debates surrounding surveillance, such as the regulation and use of encryption technologies; this is quite evident in our discourse analysis. In the following section, we therefore turn to a semiological treatment of the rhetoric of the Crypto Wars to help unveil the mythic representations of racialized populations which prove foundational for understanding the rhetorical tactics of both state and private sector actors as they negotiate the political reality of regulating encryption technology.

A semiology of the Crypto Wars

Policy debates over encryption are often leavened with mythological language by all concerned to more provocatively ground arguments made by state actors for the intrinsic security risks of unfettered cryptographic technology and, conversely, those made by private sector actors for less restrictive regulations in order to maintain competitive advantage in the global market. The mythological language used is entirely premised on representing long-standing totemic figures which encapsulate deviant stereotypes common of racialized populations, rearticulated within the context of encryption, digital communication, and the security threats they represent. Here, we use mythology as articulated by Roland Barthes (2006, pp. 114–115), for whom:

> [myth] is constructed from a semiological chain which existed before it: it is a second-order semiological system. That which is a sign (namely the associative total of a concept and an image) in the first system, becomes a mere signifier in the second. We must here recall that the materials of mythical speech [...] are reduced to a pure signifying function as soon as they are caught by myth. Myth sees in them only the raw material; their unity is that they all come down to the status of a mere language. Whether it deals with alphabetical or pictorial writing, myth wants to see in them only a sum of signs, a global sign, the final term of a first semiological chain [...] As a total of linguistic signs, the meaning of the myth has its own value, it belongs to a history [...] The meaning is already complete, it postulates a kind of knowledge, a past, a memory, a comparative order of facts, ideas, decisions.

In brief, myth is generated when a preexistent sign is associated with an artificed meaning for particular groups, places, and times via its successful assertion within the politics of a given milieu, thereby becoming successfully embedded and legible for certain cultures. The bespoke nature of myth means that its durability and reach is an idiosyncratic function of its cultural circulation. Myth is a constantly generative order of language, with new associations always being fabricated, some fading, and all having to constantly renew themselves to maintain their cultural legibility. When we are considering discourse, then we must consider the way in which mythological knowledge, these ever-evolving and dynamic second-order semiotic associations circulating as part of the experience of language, serves as an influential component that must be confronted when considering the "problem of the 'discursive regime,' of the effects of power peculiar to the play of statements" (Foucault, 2010, p. 55).

Myths regarding the Other are one of the most durable, indeed perennial, and influential forms of myth which circulate in human cultures. Such myths are so persistent in their various permutations that it is entirely possible that there is always "a set of people who, in one way or another, are regarded as pertaining to the foreigner, members of a surplus population, undesirables of whom one hopes to be rid"

(Mbembe, 2019, p. 42). The recitation of these myths regarding the other, the despised populations which may represent absolute threat and for whom "death has nothing tragic about it" and is "deprived of all symbolism" is the semiotic motor of what Achille Mbembe calls the necropolitical, an ascendant form of powers premised on the normalization of death for groups at the margins of society, whether by large-scale destruction of "the strategy of 'small massacres' inflicted one day at a time, using an implacable logic of separation, strangulation, and vivisection, as we see in all the contemporary theaters of terror and counterterror" (Mbembe, 2019, p. 38). Each time a stereotype is successfully deployed in everyday or political speech, it is another mark of the necropolitical, as "racism is the driver of necropolitical principle insofar as it stands for organized destruction, for a sacrificial economy" (Mbembe, 2019, p. 38). When myths regarding the criminal nature of racialized populations are used to justify policy, and especially when they are effective, it not only signifies the potent renewal of that myth as a legible form of inferential language, but further drives the necropolitical abuse of the subjects whose lives are rendered fodder for the promotion of state power.

It is difficult to overstate the role such myths play in the Crypto Wars. Within these debates, mythological language bridges the reciprocal, mutually reinforcing movement between older, pre-digital mythologies regarding perennial enemies of national and state security—the pantheon of contemporary criminal others who serve as the landscape of perceived threat in security debates—alongside an emergent mythology regarding the unprecedented dangers inherent in digital technologies. Myths concerning the fundamental insecurity of the commercialized internet buttress antecedent mythological concepts of racialized criminals, who are depicted in such arguments as naturally gravitating toward encryption to cover up their deviant, criminal (often violent and sexual) activities; conversely, the presumptive uptake of encryption by these archetypal enemies of the US simultaneously underscores and augments the perceived threat of such technologies, doubly underlining the need for an extraordinary response to this alignment of old and new threats. For their part, private sector technology firms mobilized similar mythological language while constructing a different threat: that of the foreign country which could dominate economic globalization, becoming a threat to US national security and its economic prosperity. Reevaluating the rhetoric of the Crypto Wars through the lens of mythological archetypes and their mobilization reveals the Crypto Wars as yet another necropolitical theater which strategically leverages certain racialized populations as reductive archetypes to serve as discursive resources which aid in negotiating the expansion of state as well as private sector power and to reinforce both the legibility and potency of the archetypes themselves.

Proposals for regulating encryption: mythologies of domestic criminals

The fear of racialized criminals using the capacities of the internet with unrestricted encryption is the overarching mythological construct guiding the arguments for the necessity of state intervention in the development of encryption technologies. Many state actors consistently depict encryption as fundamentally compromising law enforcement; Rep. Edward Markey, for example, questioned whether:

> technology is evolving at such a rapid pace that it has surpassed our ability to be able to provide the police with an adequate ability to be able to monitor, through legal court order, the conversations, the information which is being transmitted over these modern technologies.
>
> (Telecommunications Network Security, 1993)

Over the course of debates over encryption regulation, these theoretical concerns become increasingly framed as a concrete inevitability given the spread and saturation of digital technologies in different areas of life. As Robert Litt of the Department of Justice stated:

> I can't emphasize too strongly the danger that unbreakable, non-recoverable encryption poses: as we move further into the digital age, as more and more data is stored electronically rather than on paper, as very strong encryption becomes built into more and more applications, and as it becomes easier and easier to use encryption as a matter of routine, our national security and public safety will be endangered unless we act responsibly.
>
> (United States Senate, 1998)

The commercialization of the internet and its availability in more accessible, user-friendly forms, is used by Litt to argue that criminals of any technical sophistication will quickly be able to exploit cryptographic technologies to commit violent, organized (often sexual or drug-related) crime. The use of encryption by criminal groups who are historically racialized (cf. Kappeler and Potter, 2018) is not merely framed as an assault on the very capacity for law enforcement, but, because such interventions are always framed as fully legal and court-approved, "begins removing the power that society has given the courts," as the deputy director of the National Security Agency (NSA), William Crowell, put it (Encryption, Key Recovery, and Privacy, 1997). In this view, the mere existence of unrestricted encryption constitutes an assault on the legal system and the state as such to determine legal search and seizure activities by law enforcement agencies, while practically "stripping law enforcement of their ability to successfully perform electronic surveillance, wiretaps, and the search and seizure of criminal information stored in computers," according to Gene Voegtlin of the International Association of Chiefs of Police (Encryption Security, 1999).

State representatives invoke a set of possible criminal activities that could occur via encrypted channels, and although debates about encryption policy in the internet era have lasted more than 30 years, the set remains remarkably stable. Between 1990 and 2016, state representatives claimed encryption was used by "terrorists, drug dealers, and other criminals" and "gang members [and] drug dealers" (Telecommunications Network Security, 1993); "drug traffickers, organized crime groups, major street gangs and terrorist groups," "criminal organizations," "criminal elements or foreign agents," "sophisticated criminal[s]," and "well-organized, well-directed, well-motivated terrorist group[s] coming from abroad" (The Administration's Clipper Chip, 1994); "bad guys" and "terrorists, violent criminals, organized crime groups, and drug trafficking organizations, which are highly structured" (Communications and Computer Surveillance, 1994); "criminals, drug lords, and terrorists [...] [and] their criminal associates" and "the People's Liberation Army of China" (Encryption Security, 1999); "the criminal element" and "a massive drug dealer, an arms trafficker, a child pornographer, or a child molester" (Going Dark, 2011); "pedophiles" (Federal Bureau of Investigation, 2011); "extremists" (Terrorism Gone Viral, 2015); and "criminal defendants in every jurisdiction of America" (Going Dark, 2015).

Furthermore, encryption was depicted as being used in the commission of crimes such as "gambling, prostitution, vice, just all sorts of crime" (Telecommunications Network Security, 1993); "the drug trade" (Encryption Security, 1999); "child abduction, child exploitation, prison escape, and other threats to public safety" (Going Dark, 2011); "child pornography" (Federal Bureau of Investigation, 2011); by the Islamic State of Iraq and Syria (ISIS) to "recruit fighters, share intelligence, raise funds, and potentially plot and direct attacks undetected," to provide "advice for traveling to terror safe havens, contact information for smugglers in Turkey, or the membership process for joining ISIS itself," and as a "free zone by which to recruit, radicalize, plot, and plan" (Terrorism Gone Viral, 2015); and to "covertly plot violent robberies, murders, and kidnappings [...] to establish virtual communities to buy, sell, and encourage the creation of new depictions of horrific sexual abuse of children" (Going Dark, 2015).

At the same time, however, state officials depicted those criminals who might use encryption as potentially dangerous, crafty, and highly organized and motivated, as also being "stupid" and "lazy." One of the most common criticisms of government surveillance proposals was that criminals, if faced with a choice between a cell phone with built-in police surveillance capabilities and one without would obviously purchase the latter or would simply add their own layer of encryption to obstruct government surveillance. In response, state officials explained that criminals would buy these surveillance-enabled devices regardless. William Reinsch, Undersecretary of Commerce, told Congress to "never underestimate the stupidity of some of the people we have to deal with" (Encryption Security, 1999). Valerie Caproni, Federal Bureau of Investigation (FBI) General Counsel, made a similar comment over a decade later: "sometimes we want to think that criminals are a lot smarter than they really are. Criminals tend to be somewhat lazy, and a lot of times, they will resort to what is easy" (Going Dark, 2011). The seemingly contradictory characterization of criminals as being both "well-organized and highly-motivated" and "lazy" is not actually contradictory at all: it permits white Americans to fear racialized criminals while still believing in their own superiority and to have the confidence that law enforcement, if given enough power, can catch and incarcerate them.

These extreme views regarding the threat of malicious activity is rooted in a dual mythology regarding the internet, encryption, and highly capable criminals, whom Paul Ohm (2008, p. 1365) refers to as mythical "superusers":

> We fear the Internet on several levels. First, we fear that the world is becoming less comprehensible to the average person. We fear that increasing technological complexity masks terrifying fragility: the world seems one cascading failure away from being unplugged, taking away all of the essential services we have migrated online in the past decade. Second, we fear malicious Superusers on the Internet for several reasons. We imagine the Internet teeming with all kinds of evildoers, from simple predators to 'Supercriminal' Superusers, such as organized crime figures, terrorists, and war fighters.

The sweep of the internet over essential, everyday infrastructure and its fragile, coded nature makes it an exceptional target for wreaking havoc by either disrupting it as such or, in the case of superusers, utilizing its instrumental abilities for malicious ends. When FBI Director Louis Freeh speaks of "some [criminal] organizations, particularly the large ones [...] not only hiring their own software engineers, but [building] encrypted networks and global satellite communications to defeat our ability to access their criminal conversations with a court order" (Enforcement of Federal Drug Law, 1995), they are marshaling not only preexistent mythological language about the sophistication and pernicious reach of organized crime, but a nascent set of mythological concepts regarding the uniquely threatening environs of the internet as a space where racialized others neutralize the rule of law. The synthesis of this relatively recent mythology with far older mythological figures of crime and disorder serves not only to reinforce the threatening atmosphere of the internet but provides a new lens through which to magnify the purported threat of certain evergreen figures in the discourse of national security threats. Due to the constitution of these figures as racialized others, we see how a debate about cryptography, perhaps seemingly far afield from the racial politics of the American carceral system and its logics, in fact represents a new frontier through which such logics may be rearticulated and emboldened.

Proposals for deregulating encryption: mythologies of foreign hackers

In contrast to the police, intelligence, and congresspersons, who depict encryption as a threat to domestic social order because it harbors groups populated by racialized others and helps facilitate their deviant, criminal activity, corporations and digital rights advocates conceptualize encryption as crucial to ensuring America's economic hegemony and, by extension, protecting critical infrastructure and American industry from "unfriendly" foreign governments and their national corporations. In this understanding, the primary threat to the American people is not drug traffickers, gangs, or pedophiles, but the possibility of a globalized economy not headed by the US.

We can see these economic concerns clearly prioritized in the ways that industry representatives, digital rights advocates, and some policy makers conceptualize the relationship between encryption and crime. Although many acknowledge that encryption could potentially harbor deviant, criminal activity online, they insisted that the greater threat to US national security actually comes from foreign countries and corporations—a new threat that has emerged due to globalization. Now that companies were outsourcing labor and subcontracting with foreign companies and international subsidiaries to take advantage of regional differences in the cost of labor and capital, they were more susceptible to foreign spying, corporate and industrial espionage, fraud, and hackers. Joseph Kretz of the FMC Corporation drew an explicit connection between globalization, US economic hegemony, and the need to deregulate encryption:

> Competitive pressures are forcing businesses like FMC to work even more closely with suppliers, joint venture partners, and customers in an extended enterprise mode. This means that valuable proprietary designs, R&D data, and other strategic business information are constantly being transmitted and stored electronically around the world. This information must be protected if U.S. businesses are to remain competitive.
>
> (Encryption, 1997)

R. Patrick Watson of Eastman Kodak Company also raised the possibility that "foreign governments" could "monitor the legitimate activities of U.S. corporations and steal intellectual property for the benefit of national companies" (The Encryption Debate, 1997). The implication of these statements is that the US government's insistence on regulating encryption could prevent companies from dominating worldwide markets. Similarly, expert witnesses often argue that regulating encryption—specifically, imposing strict export controls which prevented US companies from selling products in international markets if they contained encryption—would make US companies less competitive, thus giving the upper hand to foreign firms. James Bidzos, president of RSA Data Security, Inc. suggested that:

> There is a product in South Africa that brags about being compatible with products in the U.S. The thing that I fear is that, once everybody starts to realize that they can buy a product outside the United States that is compatible with what they can get inside the United States, the next step might be for those products to become incompatible and for that overseas company to use encryption as a way to kind of get to the stop of the hill with this, and then use it as a way to throw us off by simply changing their product so it is no longer compatible.
>
> (S. 1726, 1996)

The concern here is not simply with the competitiveness of American firms, but with their ability to set the technical standards early in the market's formation and thus solidify their power over economic production by controlling the underlying technical standards governing digital products. In this view, if American companies are not able to dominate digital markets (both online marketplaces and markets for digital products) early, they will permanently lose their ability to define the parameters and direction of these markets in the future, thus getting locked into an indefinite subordinate position relative to foreign countries.

The private sector consistently argues that economic espionage and intellectual property theft by foreign governments and companies not only impacts American businesses but damages American national security as well. For many of the speakers, American economic hegemony is a precondition for a healthy domestic democracy; if American companies lose out to foreign competitors, Americans will lose their jobs, be forced to depend on foreign products, and will therefore be subjected to the whims of foreign interests. Senator Patrick Leahy argues that:

> if we maintain current controls on encryption technology, then we lose control of the market. That means American companies, by the end of the year 2000, could lose $30 billion to $60 billion—the loss of almost 200,000 jobs at a time when, Mr. Chairman, we know that these high-tech jobs are the new jobs of the future.
>
> (S. 1726, 1996)

Rep. Smith reiterated this point a few years later:

> E-commerce, the internet, all of that is becoming the leader, the driving force in our economy that is going to determine how strong our economy is, how high unemployment is, whether or not my constituents or anybody else's constituents are able to get jobs. Us continuing to be the leaders in the IT economy is about the most important issue to people's economic security as anything out there.
>
> (U.S. Encryption Policy, 1999)

Industry representatives, digital rights advocates, and policy makers who pushed for deregulating encryption habitually argued that encryption was crucial to ensuring American economic hegemony in the wake of globalization by protecting American people and companies from foreign countries. The speakers addressed (and in some instances, leveraged) widespread anxieties about future globalization as well as lingering past anxieties of Cold War espionage by depicting encryption as a technological fix that could protect the US from foreign powers. This rhetoric is premised on a mythology of omission: most crime, including corporate espionage and other economic crimes, is not a function of foreign interference but occurs internally to corporations or by domestic competitors; this pattern of selectively emphasizing certain categories of crime and excluding others wholesale is, in many instances, the sine qua non of constructing myths regarding crime.

Accommodating mythologies: a compromise between the US Government and its firms

Eventually, the Clinton administration and American IT firms reached a compromise. The government dropped its proposals to regulate encryption and agreed to lift export controls on encryption, allowing companies to sell their products with encryption abroad—and, by extension, expanding their user base and dominating global IT markets. However, we know from the Snowden disclosures that during this time, police and intelligence agencies brokered informal, backroom agreements with tech firms to ensure access to users' encrypted data and communications (e.g., Greenwald et al., 2013). We can see this incipient agreement in the 1990s congressional hearings, where congresspersons and IT company representatives argued that American corporations would work with law enforcement absent regulation—and in fact that would be an ideal situation for the government, because they would be able to carve out a significant portion of the global IT market, ensuring that as many people as possible were using American products, thus granting police and intelligence agencies even greater surveillance capabilities. For example, James Bidzos of RSA Security suggested that American companies could be trusted to maintain their own methods for accessing their customers' encrypted communications:

> The company can get into there in an emergency. Companies will want to do that. Companies will deploy encryption when they have their own emergency access available to them and the government always has recourse with a court order to go in and demand information in that way.

A year later, Ed Black, president of the Computer Communications Industry Association, reiterated this sentiment, stating that

"the administration's approach is, in essence, top-down industrial policy. Key recovery should not, and we do not think can be,
government-driven. It needs to be market-driven" (Encryption, 1997).

Speakers often argue that a market-driven approach to ensuring the
government retains access to encrypted communications could benefit the state by ensuring more users trusted digital technologies. US
citizens, the argument went, do not trust their government but they
do trust technology firms. If the latter are permitted to maintain their
own access to their users' encrypted communications, users would be
more likely to buy their products, thus ensuring the government had
more access to communications. As James Lucier—sitting in for the
president of Americans for Tax Reform, Grover Norquist—put it, "an
encryption system that is not trusted by the marketplace is just not
going to be used by anyone [...] Basically, in our view, key escrow, as it
proposed right now, is an absolute showstopper for digital commerce"
(S. 1726, 1996). Similarly, Rep. Sonny Bono stated that:

> There's all this mystery about these agencies. That mystery has to be
> cleared up because it leaves a huge question mark in the minds of the
> public. I'm not prepared to give any agency more authority when I
> don't trust it. Frankly, I don't trust any of them—we're investigating
> the INS for releasing prisoners and other crimes. It's very nice to
> have this technical rhetoric we're having, but I would not be com-
> fortable, nor would I even consider giving agencies more author-
> ity until they displaced more prudence in how they go about what
> they're supposed to do, as far as it's concerned with public safety.
> (Security and Freedom Through Encryption Act, 1996)

A year later, Rep. Sherman remarked that some people "might even trust
Bill Gates with an extra copy of the key, but none of the people who have
written me want to entrust the government with the key" (Encryption:
Individual Right to Privacy, 1997). In essence, opponents of government
proposals to ensure access to encrypted communications argue that
people simply do not trust the government to appropriately decide when
to access users' information, but they *do* trust tech firms with the same
responsibility. American technology companies are seen by these actors
as much more trustworthy when it comes to deciding when they should
and should not decrypt their customers' communications.

In fact, corporate representatives and some policy makers insist
that American technology companies would voluntarily work with the
US government to ensure they could access user data in the absence
of legislation demanding they do so. Roel Pieper, President and Chief

Executive Officer (CEO) of Tandem Computers, reminded Congress that "We, U.S. companies, must be able to compete," but assured them that "if we can compete, you can trust us that we will work with all the established security agencies around the world to then allow them to do their job with these technologies" (S. 1726, 1996). The benefits of this informal, voluntary relationship would be severely diminished, however, if foreign companies came to dominate global technology markets. Roberta Katz of Netscape Communications Corporation states that:

> If America does lose this leadership, America's law enforcement and national security interests will be further compromised. While today American law enforcement can and actually does consult with American companies as the leaders in encryption technology, they will not be able to do this if, in fact, leadership in this area passes to foreign companies. We must keep in mind that the Internet is a global medium designed to facilitate cross-country communication. Surely, it is in America's interest for American companies to remain the encryption leaders, and this can only happen if American companies can meet the demand of the global marketplace.
>
> (Security and Freedom Through Encryption Act, 1996)

Later, in the same hearing, Katz reiterates that "if American companies lose their leadership in this area, as I said before, ultimately we harm our law enforcement and national security interests because the setting of the standards will move to foreign shores."

The argument here is that the private sector should be permitted to maintain their own encryption architecture while cooperating with law enforcement and intelligence to ensure they continue to have access to users' communications. Rep. Lofgren went so far as to call domestic companies "good Americans and patriots" who will "want to work with America in an appropriate fashion to do what they can" if "there is a threat to this country"; she later stated that Silicon Valley is full of "patriotic Americans who hate crime as much as you and I and can be counted on to act in appropriate ways" (Security and Freedom Through Encryption, 1997). In the same hearing, Rep. Goodlatte posed the following hypothetical question:

> Which is better from a national security standpoint: have U.S. companies creating the most up-to-the-minute encryption technology and applying it to software, or having foreign companies

create that encryption technology? It seems to me we are better off in terms of our ability to work with the system to have it created in this country, rather than to have the Russians [...] It makes no sense to have Russians creating cryptography that we are going to use in this country. If there is going to be weak points in it, access to it, who is most likely to know about it, the U.S. government or the Russian government?

Similarly, Rep. Kennedy argues that:

in this tech area, I think that we need to co-opt, if you will, American high technology because we are the leaders in the world. The fact of the matter is if we are going to intend to be the leaders in the world for our national security purposes, it seems to me we want to work with them and make sure that this stuff is going to be sold anyway, why not make sure they are on our side? If the product is being sold all over the world, why not make sure it is our product, domestic companies that have some allegiance and some interest in this country because they know about and appreciate the values of this great country of ours.

(U.S. Encryption Policy, 1999)

In short, proponents of deregulating encryption—by lifting export bans on digital products with encryption and by dropping federal proposals for a government-run key management infrastructure—position the technology industry as patriotic partners of American carceral institutions. Far from pushing back against the racist depictions of criminals which speakers mobilized to consolidate support for increased government surveillance, privacy advocates and industry representatives accepted the underlying logic of the government's proposals: that there is a massive crime problem that needs to be dealt with.

Encryption, race, and predatory inclusion

At the outset, the Crypto Wars appear to have been fought between two sides: those pushing for increased government surveillance of all Americans and those fighting these proposals to protect individual privacy, with the state favoring the enrichment of its own power and the private sector loosely aligned with activists because of concerns about increased costs, decreased competitiveness, and ill will among consumers generated by their participation in encryption regulation. This understanding is not only reductive in its consideration of the negotiations of the state and the private sector, but risks obviating the role of race as a constitutive force driving encryption policy by framing it in the generalized terms of its outcomes for the state and the private sector without considering the rhetorical tactics which are mobilized throughout. For their part, state actors pathologically invoked mythological constructions of profoundly racialized criminal archetypes—especially gang members, terrorists, and sexual predators—to argue that the communicational reach of the internet, in concert with unfettered encryption, threatens to intensify violence, terror, and disruptions to social order. IT firms conjured images of foreign governments employing spies and hackers who wish to destroy American infrastructure, all in service of bolstering their national corporations. In the private sector's account, these foreign others—depicted as a cabalistic set who refuse to follow the rules of global market capitalism by using state resources to give their firms an unfair competitive advantage—threatens to reverse the ostensible victory of capitalism in the Cold War by hamstringing American companies in the global market, resulting in the US becoming economically dependent on other nations.

Both private sector and state actors advocated for their own interests during the Crypto Wars through constant recourse to mythological constructs, especially popular to the American imagination, concerning highly racialized and archetypal criminal figures. The new threat environment of the internet—itself a mythologized space founded on the contingency of insecurity and superpowered hackers, thereby understood to constitute an unprecedented threat environment—provides a second mythology enabling a mutually reinforcing mythic rhetoric wherein these archetypal criminal figures are further emboldened and empowered through the capabilities offered by the internet and unregulated encryption; conversely, these figures themselves provide an ideal population to rhetorically justify the need for extraordinary policing powers and strong regulation of encryption. Given the clear lineage of racialization in the establishment of the archetypes used most frequently and vociferously in these debates, the rhetoric of the Crypto Wars is, in no small part, a new permutation of preexistent processes of racializing criminal mythologization.

We argue that the Crypto Wars was a space for negotiating the conflicting logics of America's carceral institutions and an emergent network capitalism. Cottom (2020: 3) articulates a key reason why these two logics come into conflict: the internet's tendency toward expansion comes up against racism's desire to exclude, devalue, and stratify. Companies selling digital products become more profitable as their user base expands—hence why the industry tends toward monopolization (Hindman, 2018). But racist, white supremacist American institutions have long been concerned with excluding people of color, whether from housing, finance, education, or politics. Cottom (2020: 3) argues that one way in which racial capitalism and platform capitalism are accommodated is through predatory inclusion: "the logic, organization, and technique of including marginalized consumer-citizens into ostensibly democratizing mobility schemes on extractive terms." The concept of predatory inclusion has been applied to understanding racial stratification in housing (Taylor, 2019) and debt (Seamster and Charron-Chénier, 2017). A key element of predatory inclusion is that it refers to the extractive, punitive inclusion of groups who were previously excluded from mechanisms of upward mobility that have historically been available to white people.

The Crypto Wars happened alongside the Clinton administration's transformation of technology policy into poverty policy (Greene, 2021). Greene (2021, p. 31) points out a "core contradiction" in US poverty policy, similar to that articulated by Cottom (2020):

> On the one hand, the neoliberal state must offer promise: with the right skills, the global labor market becomes a space of unlimited potential where anyone can become an entrepreneur. On the other hand, the neoliberal state must threaten punishment: anyone who steps out of line will, at best, have their state support revoked or, at worst, be incarcerated.

The Clinton administration resolved this contradiction by developing a new political common sense Greene (2021, p. 5) calls the "access doctrine" or the belief that "the problem of poverty can be solved through the provision of new technologies and technical skills, giving those left out of the information economy the chance to catch up and compete." The salience of this common sense has shaped our understanding of the relationship between the internet, the economy, and poverty to the point that institutions draw upon the access doctrine to secure legitimacy and resources, often "[turning] toward technology provision and skills-training programs because these garner economic and political support and make the problems they face more manageable" (Greene, 2021, p. 15), a process Greene calls "bootstrapping." In some ways, bootstrapping resembles predatory inclusion, in that both involve "the extension of long-withheld opportunities or resources for marginalized groups who seek social mobility, but on terms that disadvantage them in the long term and eventually reproduce inter-group inequality" (Greene, 2021, p. 169).

Can the Crypto Wars be conceived in similar terms? The regulatory debates of the early 1990s marked a critical juncture in which the US federal government and American IT firms negotiated how to best include people of color in the burgeoning information economy. The American state, particularly police and intelligence agencies, wanted to prevent people of color from using strong encryption tools so that they could continue to police these communities; American IT firms, however, wanted to dominate global markets to prevent foreign countries from having control over international standards and infrastructure, while at the same time expanding their user base to include not only people of color in the US, but abroad as well. The eventual compromise these two sides reached—in which encryption was deregulated but law enforcement retained access to user data via informal, backdoor agreements—was crucial in setting the stage for the surveillance infrastructure in place today. In the late 1990s, the US government dropped their proposals for encryption regulation while lifting export controls which prevented American companies from selling their products abroad. We have learned from the Snowden disclosures that shortly thereafter, many American companies entered informal, backdoor arrangements with tech firms to gain access to users' encrypted data (Ball et al., 2018; Gallagher and Moltke, 2018; Greenwald et al., 2013). Such agreements have been critical to the police and intelligence agencies' ability to conduct surveillance of people of color both inside and outside the US.

Conclusion

National discourses on encryption regulation have remained remarkably stable over time. Catherine De Bolle and Cyrus R. Vance, Jr. (2021)—the executive director of Europol and the district attorney of New York County, respectively—recently published an article titled "The Last Refuge of the Criminal: Encrypted Smartphones." In it, they claim that "organized crime, terrorists, and child abusers are all drawn to devices and communication platforms that are designed to be technically impossible for law enforcement to law enforcement access." They go on to state that the Manhattan District Attorney was "hampered in accessing evidence in a recent child sex trafficking case, which should have provided important leads that could have saved additional trafficked children and found potential co-conspirators." The fact that these statements are indistinguishable from comments made 30 years ago suggests that there is an extremely effective and limited discursive condition at work where state arguments regarding encryption are concerned. The axiomatic set of beliefs underwriting this discursive condition, that is, the maintenance of immutable state dominance in all domains of law enforcement, leads to an essentially cyclical rhetoric which confronts new developments in encryption technology—and the radically shifting political contexts in which it is used—with uncannily identical tactics because of the fundamentally unchanging and relatively simplistic disposition regarding the absolute conservation of state juridical authority which constitutes its logic. The path of least resistance for this conservation of authority is the recurrent association of technologies which could fundamentally undercut state law enforcement capacities with the most well-established pantheon of criminal others at its disposal.

This presents an important opportunity for countersurveillance advocates and scholars to center race in their campaigns and analyses. The stability of national crypto discourses suggests that we are, in many ways, still grappling with the same questions we faced in the 1990s. As we continue to respond to police and intelligence agencies' calls for mandatory decryption capabilities, scholars and advocates could take this as an opportunity to question the underlying carceral and neoliberal logics motivating national technology policy. As vociferous calls for abolition echo from the streets into our institutions and into academia, we can no longer claim ignorance to the "unintended consequences" of our analyses (Parvin and Pollock, 2020). Rather, we need to seriously and thoroughly engage with how America's history of racism and white supremacy have and continue to structure technology policy as well as predominant critiques of it.

References

Aouragh, M., Gürses, S., Rocha, J., & Snelting, F. (2015). Let's First Get Things Done! On Division of Labour and Techno-political Practices of Delegation in Times of Crisis. *The Fibreculture Journal, 26*, 208–235.

Ball, J., Borger, J., & Greenwald, G. (2018). Revealed: How the US and UK Spy Agencies Defeat Internet Privacy and Security. *The Guardian*. https://www.theguardian.com/world/2013/sep/05/nsa-gchq-encryption-codes-security

Barthes, R., Lavers, A., & Barthes, R. (2006). *Mythologies*. Hill and Wang.

Browne, S. (2015). *Dark matters: On the surveillance of blackness*. Duke University Press.

Cottom, T. M. (2020). Where Platform Capitalism and Racial Capitalism Meet: The Sociology of Race and Racism in the Digital Society. *Sociology of Race and Ethnicity, 6*(4), 1–9.

De Bolle, C. & Vance C.R. (2021). The Last Refuge of the Criminal: Encrypted Smartphones. *Politico*. https://www.politico.eu/article/the-last-refuge-of-the-criminal-encrypted-smartphones-data-privacy

Dencik, L., Hintz, A., & Cable, J. (2016). Towards Data Justice? The Ambiguity of Anti-surveillance Resistance in Political Activism. *Big Data & Society*, *3*(2).

Foucault, M. (2010). Truth and Power. In *The Foucault Reader* (P. Rabinow, ed., pp. 51–75). New York: Vintage Books.

Gallagher, R., & Moltke, H. (2018). The Wiretap Rooms: The NSA's Hidden Spy Hubs in Eight U.S. Cities. *The Intercept*. https://theintercept.com/2018/06/25/att-internet-nsa-spy-hubs/

Greene, D. (2021). *The Promise of Access: Technology, Inequality, and the Political Economy of Hope*. Cambridge, MA: The MIT Press.

Greenwald, G., MacAskill, E., Poitras, L., Ackerman, S., & Rushe, D. (2013). Microsoft Handed the NSA Access to Encrypted Messages. *The Guardian*. https://www.theguardian.com/world/2013/jul/11/microsoft-nsa-collaboration-user-data

Gürses, S., Kundnani, A., & Van Hoboken, J. (2016). Crypto and Empire: The Contradictions of Counter-surveillance Advocacy. *Media, Culture & Society*, *38*(4), 576–590.

Hindman, M. (2018). *The Internet Trap: How the Digital Economy Builds Monopolies and Undermines Democracy*. Princeton: Princeton University Press.

Kappeler, V. E., & Potter, G. W. (2018). *The Mythology of Crime and Criminal Justice* (Fifth edition). Long Grove, IL: Waveland Press.

Kaye, D. (2015). *Report of the Special Rapporteur on the Promotion and Protection of the Right to Freedom of Opinion and Expression* (pp. 1–21). United Nations.

Mbembe, A. (2019). *Necropolitics* (S. Corcoran, Trans.). Durham: Duke University Press.

McLaughlin, J. (2015). Exclusive: Edward Snowden Explains Why Apple Should Continue to Fight the Government on Encryption. *The Intercept*. https://theintercept.com/2015/07/31/exclusive-edward-snowden-says-obama-administrations-war-encryption-just-doesnt-make-sense/

Ohm, P. (2008). The Myth of the Superuser: Fear, Risk, and Harm Online. *UC Davis Law Review*, *41*(4), 1327–1402.

Parvin, N., & Pollock, A. (2020). Unintended by Design: On the Political Uses of "Unintended Consequences." *Engaging Science, Technology, and Society*, *6*, 320–327.

Rexhepi, P. (2016). Liberal Luxury: Decentering Snowden, Surveillance and Privilege. *Big Data & Society*, *2*, 1–3.

Seamster, L., & Charron-Chénier, R. (2017). Predatory Inclusion and Education Debt: Rethinking the Racial Wealth Gap. *Social Currents*, *4*(3), 199–207.

Stevens, A., & Allen-Robertson, J. (2021). Encrypting Human Rights: The Intertwining of Resistant Voices in the UK State Surveillance Debate. *Big Data & Society*, *8*(1), 1–15.

Taylor, K.-Y. (2019). *Race for Profit: How Banks and the Real Estate Industry Undermined Black Homeownership*. The University of North Carolina Press.

United States House of Representatives (1993). *Telecommunications Network Security*.

United States House of Representatives (1994). *Communications and Computer Surveillance, Privacy and Security.*

United States House of Representatives (1995). *Enforcement of Federal Drug Laws: Strategies and Policies of the FBI and DEA.*

United States House of Representatives (1996). *Security and Freedom through Encryption (SAFE) Act.*

United States House of Representatives, 1 (1997). *Encryption: Individual Right to Privacy vs. National Security.*

United States House of Representatives (1997). *The Security and Freedom Through Encryption (SAFE) Act.*

United States House of Representatives (1999). *Encryption Security in a High Tech Era.*

United States House of Representatives (1999). *U.S. Encryption Policy.*

United States House of Representatives (2011). *Federal Bureau of Investigation.*

United States House of Representatives (2011). *Going Dark: Lawful Electronic Surveillance in the Face of New Technologies.*

United States House of Representatives (2015). *Terrorism Gone Viral: The Attack in Garland, Texas, and Beyond.*

United States Senate (1994). *The Administration's Clipper Chip Key Escrow Encryption Program.*

United States Senate (1996). *S. 1726, The Promotion of Commerce Online in the Digital Era Act of 1996, or "PRO-CODE" Act.*

United States Senate (1997). *Encryption.*

United States Senate (1997). *The Encryption Debate: Criminals, Terrorists, and the Security Needs of Business and Industry.*

United States Senate (1997). *Encryption, Key Recovery, and Privacy Protection in the Information Age.*

United States Senate (1998). *Privacy in the Digital Age: Encryption and Mandatory Access.*

United States Senate (2015). *Going Dark: Encryption, Technology, and the Balance Between Public Safety and Privacy.*

West, S. M. (2018). Cryptographic Imaginaries and the Networked Public. *Internet Policy Review, 7*(2), 1–16.

West, S. M. (2021). Survival of the Cryptic: Tracing Technological Imaginaries across Ideologies, Infrastructures, and Community Practices. *New Media & Society,* Online First, 1–21.

3 Data Privacy in Digital Advertising

Towards a Post-Third-Party Cookie Era

Naim Çınar and Sezgin Ateş

Introduction

The rapid growth of data breaches and misusage, user privacy violations, the adoption of data protection, and privacy legislation in many
countries are clear signs of the growing importance of data privacy
issues, and digital advertising practices are at the heart of this complex
domain. Data privacy issues deal with how the data is acquired and
stored, what it is used for, and whether it is shared with a third party.
In most cases, these data consist of traces of the digital activities of internet users. The privacy of a human in the digital landscape is of vital
importance because whether it is online or offline privacy, it is a human
right protected by law. Moreover, the right to privacy does not relin-
quish its force while entering a digital world. In this sense, the value of
online privacy is not different from privacy in the physical world.

We humans are social beings. Each of us builds relationships to feel
a part of and function effectively in society, and sharing information
about ourselves is the natural part of this communication process. In
the physical world, we tend to watch over our privacy while exchanging
information with someone or a community or when we are involved in
personal or group activities. We are more experienced in controlling
what we hide or what we share in the physical world, but maintaining
privacy is far more complicated in the digital landscape where we are
still struggling to integrate. It is because companies are involved in the
online world. After all, they provide most of the online platforms and
other related online services. Internet users build up a vast amount of
digital footprint knowingly or unknowingly by leaving their personally
identifiable information (PII) from their everyday activities of creating,
sharing, and consuming content through online platforms. PII is:

> any information about an individual maintained by an agency,
> including (1) any information that can be used to distinguish or

DOI: 10.4324/9781003173335-3

trace an individual's identity, such as name, Social Security number, date and place of birth, mother's maiden name, or biometric records; and (2) any other information that is linked or linkable to an individual, such as medical, educational, financial, and employment information.

(United States Government Accountability
Office [GAO], 2008)

A brief history of web tracking and targeted advertising

Today, internet users are surrounded by a mixed bag of online activity trackers. As a matter of fact, the history of data protection and online privacy is as old as the history of the commercial internet. Data privacy concerns have been on a continually growing trend since commercial internet access in the mid-1990s. This trend seems to continue to grow, as digital technologies are getting more complex each day.

Two lawyers, Warren and Brandeis's (1890) essay in *Harvard Law Review* was among the first to mention the right to privacy. They defined it as the individual's right to be let alone and emphasized that it should receive added protection in the criminal law. Seventy-five years after this article, in the US, the Supreme Court first recognized the right to privacy in 1965.[1] The privacy protection laws of that period were limited in scope and the world's technological capacity to store information was in the very early stages. In 1973, US Health, Education, and Welfare Advisory Committee released *The Code of Fair Information Practices* report regarding the impact of computerization on medical record privacy. The Code was based on five principles about the privacy rights of individuals and requirements for organizations. In 1981, Council of Europe (CoE) adopted the *Convention for the Protection of Individuals with regard to Automatic Processing of Personal Data* treaty, also known as Convention 108. It was the first international treaty to address the privacy of personal data. Convention 108 is still valid today, with several amendments over time. The latest modernization of the convention was on May 18, 2018, just a week before the applicability of the EU's general data protection regulation (GDPR). The main objective of modernization was to strengthen it to deal with challenges resulting from the ongoing advancements in information and communication technologies (ICT).

In the early 1990s, the invention of two applications, Gopher[2] and the World Wide Web (WWW), paved the way for the internet to be accessible to anyone. Soon, the internet transformed into "a globe-spanning system linking millions of computers and placed them at the center of a new communications medium" (Abbate, 1999, p. 2). The advances in ICTs and the transformation of the internet in that period created new potentials for privacy violations (Turn, 1990). Data privacy had grown as a concerning issue in the later years. Nevertheless, there was digital optimism while the internet was beginning to enter our daily lives. Electronic Frontier Foundation's (EFF's) cofounder Barlow (1996)'s "A Declaration of the Independence of Cyberspace" is a well-known example of digital utopianism in the 1990s. In the manifesto, cyberspace was hailed as "a zone of sovereignty, free from the terrestrial strictures of nation, government, or law" (Ankerson, 2018, p. 96). Although this was an example of a utopian vision, there was a positive atmosphere in the early years of the commercial internet. In an interview, the creator of the Javascript programming language Brendan Eich described the early times of public access to the internet and the introduction of cookies:

> When we were working on the web in the 90s, we were not thinking ahead too far. The basic idea was to make the web useful for people. The early web was text and hyperlinks. Pretty soon, people got tired of just text and, they wanted images as well, and that led to an invented element that you could put on your page, but it referred to a different machine by its internet address... Then in 1994, the cookie came along. You could think of that as a way of saving some information in your browser for every site you visit. It was meant so when you go to your bank and sign in, you would not have to sign in every time you went forward or back or started your browser. Between the cookie and image, you had a tracking system without knowing it. We did this naively. We were saying 'let's make the web useful', 'let's put images in', 'let's make cookies so, you don't have to log in all the time.'
>
> (NBC News, 2019)

Even though the cookies were initially designed to make surfing the web easy, companies soon realized that they could set up their cookies on other websites to collect visitor profiles. The cookie controversy has always been around since its introduction, and it is still the preeminent source of online privacy concerns. Cookies are small, plain, non-executable text files stored on your browser, and they function as memory aides for websites (Data & Marketing Association, 2020). According to Cahn et al. (2016), "a cookie is a small piece of data placed on a client browser when it accesses a given server" (p. 981).

The cookie is transmitted back to that server in the header of subsequent requests. Netscape Communications developed cookies in 1994. Just a year after, Kevin O'Connor and Dwight Merriman formed the Internet Advertising Network (IAN) and started to use cookies for the first time to serve advertising interests. IAN was soon renamed Doubleclick (Reese, 2002). Their product Dynamic Advertising, Reporting, and Targeting (DART) was the first example of third-party collectors of cookies. Therefore, the history of cookies and the history of data privacy in digital advertising dates back to the same time.

In his 1996 bestseller book *Being Digital*, Nicholas Negroponte anticipated that the users would be able to personalize the digital media content. Access to the digital media content would be mostly pay-per-view, and the users and advertisers would share the costs of digital media. Ad-free digital content would also be available for a higher fee. He also anticipated that the advertising would be so personalized that it would be indistinguishable from the content (Negroponte, 1995). Some of his predictions proved correct, but "the crucial difference is that much of the content is not being customized and personalized by the users" (Turow, 2012, p. 30). Instead, digital content providers personalize the content for users with the help of online tracking technologies such as cookies, web beacons, tracking pixels, and browser fingerprinting. However, personalized user experience and free content come at a cost, and in most cases, it is paid in the form of sharing personal data with first and third parties.

The rise of first-party data

First-party and third-party trackers are the two essential elements of online tracking. European Network and Information Security Agency (ENISA) defines first-party trackers as the "websites or applications with which the user is directly interacting" (ENISA, 2012, p. 3). The websites and applications track their users with existing tracking techniques to collect user analytics data, improve user experience, and personalize services. "Several regulations even require first-party cookies to track users for purposes of fraud prevention, anti-money laundering, national security, and law enforcement" (Tene & Polenetsky, 2012, p. 305). Any data the website or application owner collects from their users is first-party data. The original purpose of using this type of dataset is to improve user experience – ease of use, consistency, clarity, security, and so on – and the services/products of the provider. The users often expect first-party data owners not to share the data with third parties. Therefore, first-party trackers should be transparent in answering the following questions. How is first-party data collected and stored? What is collected, when, and why? What is it used for? It is the necessity of a transparent data privacy policy. The collection of first-party data is a sensitive issue. Any misuse of it might damage the trust that is difficult to regain. Jebbit's (2019) consumer data trust index lists what causes US internet users to distrust a brand when providing personal information as follows: brands asking for too much information, public data scandal, inaccurate information used in marketing to the user, confusing privacy policies, and experiencing "creepy" advertising. Datagrail's (2020) consumer privacy expectations report shows that the topmost concern of US citizens about first-party data collection is if their personal information is sold to third-parties. According to Privitar's (2020) report on consumer trust and data privacy, having their data stolen as part of a data breach or security issue is the forefront reason for making consumers uncomfortable with first-party trackers collecting their data. These findings signify that most companies still fail to eliminate the consumers' concerns over first-party data collection.

Data governance[3] is the key to avoid the issues that stem from first-party data collection and ensures regulatory compliance with data privacy standards across the world (e.g., GDPR in Europe, APP[4] in Australia, PIPEDA [soon to be replaced with CPPA][5] in Canada, PDPA[6] in Singapore). Data governance is a framework that defines the roles, responsibilities, and processes regarding the generating, collecting, processing, and protection of data. It ensures the accountability of companies for their data assets. Janssen, Brous, Estevez, Barbosa, and Janowski (2020, p. 2) define data governance as: "Organizations and their personnel defining, applying and monitoring the patterns of rules and authorities for directing the proper functioning of, and ensuring the accountability for, the entire life-cycle of data and algorithms within and across organizations." Today, more companies are collecting a large amount of data from their customers with the intent of being data-driven. Data-drivenness allows them to make decisions based on actual data, but the ever-increasing number of collected data makes things more complex. As the amount of data increases, so does the responsibility for protecting personal information and demands for the company to comply with constantly updated global data privacy regulations.

The meaning and scope of personal data had been unclear, but the current data privacy regulations provided an explicit and expanded definition. Any information related to an identified or identifiable data subject – a natural person – is considered personal data under the EU's

GDPR ("What is considered personal data under the EU GDPR?," n.d.). "Any data" in the context of this definition refers to (but is not limited to) information such as names, surnames, home addresses, email addresses, identification card numbers, appearance and behaviors, geo-tracking data, internet protocol (IP) addresses, cookie IDs, data held by hospital or doctor, workplace data, educational backgrounds, religious views, and political opinions (Microsoft, 2017). This definition provides a clear framework for the responsibilities of data-driven businesses regarding the data assets they have. Therefore, it is becoming more crucial for companies to have an effective data governance program to protect the data and prevent any exposure and breaches.

Third-party data is still the primary source of creating profiles of consumers from their online activities and targeting digital advertisements. However, we are about to enter a post-third-party cookie era, and the alternative approaches and technologies replacing it are not yet clear. What is clear is that first-party data has become a much more important source for targeting consumers. According to Interactive Advertising Bureau's (IAB's) 2021 report on preparedness for the post-third-party cookie and identifier tracking system, most stakeholders involved in the digital advertising ecosystem have not yet realized that the loss of third-party data could limit reaching audiences online with precision. In the report, IAB urges these stakeholders to aggressively collect and leverage first-party data to realize its full potential because the findings show that most companies do not spend enough on the use of first-party data. Data collection is most often limited to basic data – contact, location, and employment info – and the majority of collected data is not leveraged for advertising (IAB, 2021). It is apparent that the investment in first-party data collection and in-house data management will continue to increase.

There are different ways for brands (advertisers) and publishers to collect first-party data from their website, social media platforms, applications, and data stored in customer relationship management (CRM). However, it is necessary to use a variety of technology tools to collect sophisticated first-party data effectively. Moreover, making sense of collected data is another barrier for most companies. At this point, Big Tech companies come back into the stage to maintain their presence at the center of this ecosystem by providing various solutions to help deal with first-party data. Google published an extensive report in 2020 in which they praise the rise of first-party data. The paper listed four key marketing activations that first-party data can deploy – a deep understanding of key audience segments, strategic consumer engagement, hyper-personal experiences through leveraging machine learning and analytics, and advanced cross channel lead management. Furthermore, it included how Google products, such as Analytics 360, Display & Video 360, BigQuery, Auto ML, and Ads API might help companies unleash first-party data's full potential (Boston Publishing Group [BPG] & Google, 2020). Facebook also allows businesses to use its algorithms to collect data through its services – Lead Generation and first-party cookies for Facebook Pixel. Several other big e-commerce platforms, search engines, and social media platforms have products to facilitate first-party data collection, too. There is one major drawback of utilizing from services of Big Tech. Most often, brands and publishers have limited control over their first-party data when they use the services of external partners, and they can only use it within that ecosystem. The irony here is that the cookie-free future will likely put Big Tech in a stronger position in the digital advertising universe.

Publishers – any website that creates its own content – are the other important actors in the digital advertising ecosystem. They will most likely hold even a more critical role in the post-third-party data era. Until now, most publishers have relied on third-party ad networks to serve ads, but this is about to change. Publishers have the opportunity to collect valuable personal data from their users every time they log in to view content. Advertisers are already showing interest in these data sources. For instance, the data platform of global publisher giant Condé Nast's Spire includes an extensive amount of first-party data of their customers worldwide. The platform allows advertisers to deliver personalized ads in digital channels owned by Condé Nast (Condé Nast, 2018). Some publishers even have started pooling their first-party data to create a digital ad network. Ozone Project[7] in the UK and OpenAP[8] in the US are examples of such publisher alliances which claim to provide a trusted and transparent platform for advertisers to reach their audiences in the cookie-free world. We will probably see more suchlike practices shortly soon, which means more publishers will likely build walled gardens[9] of their own, just like Big Tech companies. Bringing data in-house in the name of user privacy protection will be more prominent in the post-third-party era, and this race for first-party data appears to cause new problems. First of all, it might create a disadvantage for smaller brands and publishers because they have smaller amounts of data to work with. As a result, they might be more dependent on the infrastructure and data of walled gardens to reach their audiences. This might eventually result in more asymmetrical relationships in the advertising technology (AdTech) ecosystem. Besides, the impact of the new privacy policies of Big Tech on the AdTech ecosystem is as strong as the data privacy regulations.

The greater risk is that Big Tech might consolidate its dominance over the internet with privacy-focused updates by exploiting privacy concerns. However, we do not yet know to what extent the reconstruction in the AdTech industry to prepare for the post-third-party era will meet the rising expectations for user privacy and a more balanced relationship between the actors of the AdTech ecosystem.

A technology on the verge of extinction: third-party cookies

If we were to write this chapter only a few years ago, our primary focus would be on third-party data collection. Since its emergence, it has been the key technology in the AdTech ecosystem and the primary source of data privacy concerns. However, Google announced that it would completely phase out cookies on its browser Chrome by 2022 – later delayed the plan until 2023 (Goel, 2021). Other popular browsers such as Mozilla Firefox with its Enhanced Tracking Prevention (ETP) feature and Apple Safari with its Intelligent Tracking Prevention (ITP) feature are already blocking third-party cookies by default. Besides, Apple has updated the privacy features of its devices to give users more control over third-party tracking as a part of its privacy-focused strategy that aims to turn the increasing privacy awareness of users into a business advantage. The update, which went into effect with version 14.5 in April 2021 to Apple iOS, iPadOS, and tvOS devices, requires applications to ask their users for their permission to track them across apps and websites owned by other companies. This update provided users the right to decide whether to opt in or opt out to sharing their Apple device's unique Identifier for Advertisers (IDFA). It is an anonymized unique identifier that Apple uses to identify the user's device without revealing PII. Advertisers use it to deliver targeted advertisements and measure campaign performance. With the update, most of the users are expected to opt out of sharing IDFA. The current research on opt out rates after the Apple privacy update reveals that only 15% of the users worldwide have opted in since its launch (Flurry Analytics, 2021). Third-party data nonetheless remains a key data source. IAB's State of Data report (2021) shows that although the AdTech industry is preparing for a cookie-free future, investment in third-party data continues to grow because of the lack of understanding that third-party data will soon be a thing of the past.

Considering third-party data collection from the web remains the prominent focus of related academic research on data privacy in digital advertising, we believe it is still necessary to discuss this practice which will be obsolete soon. Third-party data is any information collected by an organization (e.g., AdTech platforms) that does not have a direct relationship with the data subject. This type of personal data being held by others has long been the bedrock of the AdTech ecosystem. However, this practice represents a potential impact on privacy. As Mayer and Mitchell (2012) state, "third-party data collection supports free content on the web and facilitates web innovation, but it comes at a privacy cost" (p. 413). Third-party data providers collect and aggregate demographic, psychographic (e.g., lifestyle, interests, personality traits), and behavioral (e.g., purchasing habits, brand interactions, webpage/app usage analytics) information about users from websites, applications, and plugins with a range of tools, including cookies, tracking pixels, browser fingerprinting, and web beacons. The fact that third-party data contains such detailed and comprehensive information about target audiences has made it an essential component for targeted advertising campaigns. Advertisers and their agencies can use third-party data for various purposes like recognizing audiences, targeting, retargeting, identifying potential targets, merging it with first-party data, gaining insights, personalization, and customization. However, consumers had little or no control over how their personal information is collected and used by third parties until the recent data privacy regulations came into effect. This power imbalance or, to be more specific, privacy asymmetry between consumers and data collectors remains a big issue in many countries where comprehensive and up-to-date data regulations do not apply.[10]

Moreover, many consumers are not even aware of the existence of most third-party data aggregators. As Roderick (2014) points out, these companies remain largely invisible to consumers despite creating a multibillion dollar industry. In his article on the commodification of personal information, Crain (2018, p. 93) provides a clear explanation of the source of the persistent transparency problem in the data broker industry by drawing attention to two significant limits of transparency. First, comprehensive transparency is practically impossible to implement, as the industry's business model is based on privacy asymmetry. The structure and the operations of the industry are incompatible with a comprehensive transparency framework. Another limit is that transparency initiatives have historically favored the self-regulation of the industry. Although the industry created an illusion of privacy in part by self-regulations, the power imbalance at the core of the ecosystem remained intact. This attitude has led to continuous violation of consumer privacy by exploiting the situation. Hence, insufficient transparency about how third parties access, collect, and sell personal data and insufficient respect for user consent in the Ad-Tech ecosystem have led to increasing consumer privacy concerns.

The AdTech industry had long defended the use of third-party data on the ground of its necessity to provide free content and personalized experiences on the internet. However, the increase in data breach scandals, growing consumer privacy concerns over the years, and the introduction of comprehensive data protection regulations across the world have accelerated the transition to the post-third-party data era. The players of the AdTech industry – Big Tech companies, data brokers, publishers, advertising agencies, industry associations – are now in a hurry to tune their business models for the new era. Besides the industry's lean towards first-party data dependent strategies, major actors of AdTech (e.g., PRAM[11]) have rolled out several alternative approaches and technologies to third-party cookies, which promise to target consumers in a personalized and meaningful manner while respecting their privacy. For instance, Google has announced a new environment called *Privacy Sandbox* to test a series of proposals such as Federated Learning of Cohorts (FLoC) and First "Locally Executed Decision over Groups" Experiment (FLEDGE) for privacy-safe ad targeting. In the FLoC[12] proposal, users are placed within cohorts based on their browsing behavior to reach them with relevant content and ads. Simply put, the idea is to allow advertisers to target a cohort of users with similar browsing histories without revealing their identities and individually tracking them. FLEDGE,[13] however, addresses the retargeting challenge. The proposal is predicated on the concept that website owner (publisher) – or even a demand-side platform (DSP) if the publisher permits[14] – can assign each website visitor's browser to an interest group based on their actions on that site. Thus, ad seller platforms can initiate an on-device bidding process to determine which ad to show based on the assigned interest groups of the user (Underwood, 2021). In this scenario, the information is stored on the user's browser, not by the advertiser or any AdTech platform. However, it is not yet clear how these technologies will work.

However, various parties have raised concerns regarding Google's proposals. One of the prominent concerns is that the Privacy Sandbox initiative could further solidify Google's dominance in the industry. Furthermore, the EFF, the leading nonprofit digital rights group, described the proposals as a way to reinvent behavioral targeting and corporate surveillance (Cyphers, 2021). Google's announcement that it is delaying its plans to phase out cookies in the Chrome browser until 2023 is a sign that it needs more time to test these proposals, persuade the AdTech industry, and ensure full compliance with GDPR and other similar data privacy regulations.

Apart from Google's proposals, the AdTech industry rolled out several open-source proposals, including Secure Web Addressability Network (SWAN)[15] and Unified ID 2.0.[16] In the SWAN proposal, when users visit a website for the first time, they will be asked to give consent for all publishers that use SWAN to show them ads (White, 2021), and their preferences will be stored as Secure Web ID (SWID), a pseudonymous identifier[17] in their browser. SWAN proposal claims that users will have full control over their data at all times, and the data within the SWAN network will only ever persist in the web browser of users. Another proposal adopted by many AdTech companies is Unified ID 2.0. It is a new form of identity-based tracking that aims to replace third-party cookies with hashed and encrypted email-based IDs. In the Unified ID 2.0 proposal, when a user logs in to a website or app with an email address, the publisher will create an identifier based on the anonymized hashed and encrypted version of that email following the user's consent. The proposal claims that a user's anonymized ID will contain zero information about who they are in the real world and users will be able to monitor and control how their data is used.

These proposals and many other similar ones (e.g., Microsoft's PARAKEET[18]) are all under development. Walled gardens and the rest of the AdTech industry are competing to determine the future of tracking on the web. Therefore, it is too early to say which one will become the dominant ad-serving technology replacing third-party cookies. On the other hand, consumers struggle to understand the complex structure of online tracking technologies and how to protect their right to digital privacy. Many are concerned about the lack of control over their personal information on the internet. For this reason, it is necessary to look at the AdTech ecosystem through the lens of corporate surveillance and the commodification of personal information to understand the dynamics of the industry from a broader perspective that includes all actors.

Confronting corporate surveillance and exploitation of consumers

Digital advertising has crossed the boundaries of advertising as we know it. The fundamental difference between traditional and digital advertising is that the AdTech industry has a vast capacity to reach limitless information about consumers that was almost impossible to reach before the digital era and uses this information to target the right consumers at the right time and place. Monitoring, collecting, accumulating, processing, and using personal data for advertising purposes is the new norm of advertising practices. However, this structural transformation and the aggressive use of personal information bring intense debates with it. At the heart of the controversy are the corporate surveillance and commodification of personal data.

Various terms such as online behavioral advertising (Smit et al., 2014), online targeted advertising (Shoenberger, 2017), online personalized advertising (Tucker, 2014), data-driven digital advertising (Aiolfi et al., 2021), tailored advertising (Turow et al., 2009), and programmatic advertising (Busch, 2016) have been used to explain data-driven online personalized ads. The AdTech industry adamantly pleads that online targeted advertising is all about delivering quality and relevant content, customized services for consumers freely, and eventually increasing the effectiveness of ads. Some studies affirm these claims and demonstrate that consumers seek out more relevant and probabilistic predictions meeting their needs and desires (Xu et al., 2011; Kumar & Gupta, 2016; Ruckenstein & Granroth, 2020). Besides, personalization increases advertising effectiveness (Bright & Daugherty, 2012; Tucker, 2012; Bleier & Eisenbeiss, 2015). However, targeted advertising strictly depends upon personal data, and the collection of personal data requires corporate surveillance that has destructive effects on consumers. Surveillance is not something newly coined, and it has been a part of our daily lives for years. But as Bernal (2016, p. 246) points out, surveillance in the digital world is far more than "analogue phone-tapping, photography, listening devices and so on." With the help of ubiquitous and elaborative surveillance, "online advertising practices have evolved from the rudimentary and ineffective pop-up and banner ads, to involuntary and invasive adware installations to more recent data-driven techniques such as collaborative filtering, contextual and personalized advertising and behavioral targeting" (Bodle, 2016, p. 139).

Several researchers (Schneier, 2015; Bernal, 2016; Bodle; 2016) discuss that surveillance in the digital era differs from the traditional one with specific aspects. First of all, in parallel with the continuous development of digital technologies, surveillance got out of governments' hands; thus, every single action of users became open and visible to the AdTech industry. Thanks to this rapid shift, advertisers, publishers, marketers, data brokers, and other intermediary firms had a chance to make sense of personal data and use it to modify consumer behavior. Their surveillance capacities have been growing day after day. Second, the information open to the AdTech industry reached incredible amounts. With the help of algorithmic methods, the AdTech industry tracks and monitors uninterruptedly what we write, what we buy, or whom we make friends or predicts our political affiliation, sexual orientation, religion, and even possible behaviors like having a baby, getting married, moving to a different country. This various information returns to us as targeted advertising. Moreover, this information that the AdTech industry gets never vanishes even if we delete or forget it. The AdTech industry has a huge capacity to store historical data and has more retentive memory than we have. Third, the effect of surveillance activities on people's lives swiftly extended. Misuse of personal data (Baek & Morimoto, 2012), data leakage (Toubiana & Verdot, 2011), hacking and identity thefts (Ruckenstein & Granroth, 2020), sharing data with third parties without permission (Ur et al., 2012), loss of personal autonomy, discrimination (Dāvida, 2020), and above all consumer privacy concerns (Phelps et al., 2001; Anton et al., 2010; McDonald & Cranor, 2010; Smit et al., 2014; Kim & Huh, 2017) are some of the prominent effects. Given that corporate surveillance involves billions of people, you can imagine the scale of these effects. Moreover, ever-growing digital technologies made the process of monitoring, tracking, collecting, aggregating, and analyzing personal data much more manageable, automatic, continuous, simple, and inexpensive for the AdTech industry more than ever. This transformation indicates that today, we are exposed to pervasive surveillance.

Data capitalism (West, 2019), surveillance capitalism (Zuboff, 2019), and dataveillance (Raley, 2013; van Dijck, 2014) are some of the terms which characterize the data and surveillance-based ecosystem we have been living in for at least the last 25 years. The fuel of corporate surveillance is the continuous data flow provided by consumers. On the strength of this limitless data flow, the AdTech industry "gets an unassailable strategic advantage in service quality, customization, message targeting, and cost reduction" (Barwise & Watkins, 2018, p. 28). It may seem that some consumers also take advantage of this process. However, with the words of Bodle (2016, p. 140), "withholding what information is known about a person and how it is used prevents people from anticipating consequences and making informed decisions." Relevant studies corroborate Bodle's words. Consumers do not even have a clear understanding of how the AdTech industry's tactics work, how they use technologies to target them, and the roles of different companies involved in the process (Ur et al., 2012; Ham, 2017). Moreover, they show little awareness of the privacy implications of data sharing or the actual scope of online targeted advertising (van Eijk et al., 2012). Under the skin, it is an unequal relationship that depends upon the exploitation of consumers' vulnerabilities. As West (2019, p. 22) remarks, "data capitalism is not just about surveillance: It is about how the market imbues data with new kinds of informational power and capitalizes upon it while rendering this power invisible in the name of transparency and consumer efficacy." The AdTech industry's plan for targeting users without exposing their identities and individually tracking them does not change the fact that they will continue to commodify personal data, manipulate consumers, and maximize their profit.

Fuchs (2012) and Zuboff (2019) argue that this surveillance-based regime created its own system of exploitation. What is being exploited is billions of internet users as free labor, and this exploitation serves the control/manipulation of people and, in the last instance, accumulation of capital. This regime that "builds its prowess on the value of data and metadata" (van Dijck, 2014, p. 199), exploits consumers' vulnerabilities, weaknesses, and emotions. It is not only personal data that is traded but also the meanings, categorizations, and insights inferred from personal data (Fourcade & Healy, 2017) under the name of delivering personalized ads. Content providers mostly offer free or below-cost products and services, and it is an undeniable fact. However, "they capture more and more personal data" (Barwise & Watkins, 2018, p. 25) and transform them into tradable objects. The commodification of personal data and exploitation of free labor gives corporate actors incredible power and dominance and creates power asymmetry between those who set the rules and those who mostly do not have any other option than to obey the rules. Consumers are the main actors of surplus value production. Even so, their control, ownership, and understanding of personal data are pretty limited (Bodle, 2016) because surveillance operations are deliberately designed to be incomprehensible and unknowable to consumers (Zuboff, 2019).

Allmer (2015) states that there is a logic behind this asymmetry. Digital content providers produce an antagonism between consumers' desire to be part of the digital world and privacy/surveillance threats. Consumers generally alternate between benefits and damages of the digital world; however, they mostly follow benefits as acquisition-transaction utility theory (Baek & Morimoto, 2012) or as social exchange theory (Schumann et al., 2014) suggests. *Privacy paradox* (Norberg et al., 2007) also refers to this antagonism. Consumers want to access the digital world and are also concerned about their privacy and loss of control over their data. Most of them sacrifice their data and run the risk of losing control over personal data. Still, some of them improve skills to protect themselves, such as providing incomplete/

wrong information (Sheehan & Hoy, 1999), deleting cookies periodically (Wills & Zeljkovic, 2011), and using ad-blocking software (Austin & Newman, 2015). On the other hand, the industry adopts the "take it or leave it" approach on the strength of its dominance in the digital world. It is not something like "sign or die" but it is close to "sign or not to live like most people" (Richards & Hartzog, 2019, p. 1488). In this process, the AdTech industry leans up consumers' consent. The main claim is that consumers enter the digital world and use the facilities by giving their consent. However, consumers do not have any bargaining power on the flip side because of the power asymmetry. For instance, as Skeggs and Yuil (2016, p. 388) exemplify, "users feel angry about Facebook making money out of their data, but they do not hesitate to contract with the devil." In this sense, consumers' consent itself becomes questionable, especially considering how consent is obtained and exploited.

According to GDPR, consent must be "freely given, specific, informed and unambiguous." In order to obtain freely given consent, it must be given voluntarily. The element "free" implies a "real" choice by the data subject ("GDPR Consent", n.d.). However, most of these requirements are not fulfilled in practice; thus, the validity of informed consent is controversial in many ways. First of all, privacy policies are unilateral, long, complex, and ambiguous documents. Consumers do not get a say in the content of policies, but they are expected to accept it unquestioningly. A study by Earp et al. (2005) indicates a significant difference between consumers' privacy expectations and what privacy policies emphasize. Besides, most consumers do not read privacy policies or comprehend the policies' content (Bruvere & Lovic, 2021) and are unaware of what is agreed to, what data practices are possible, and the potential informational risks of the transactions (Richards & Hartzog, 2019). Second, even though giving consent is based on voluntariness in appearance, it is mandatory in practice. "I do not consent" mostly means not reaching the content. In other words, consumer consent in the digital world is coerced or not a real choice. Since most consumers do not take the risk of being excluded from the digital world, they are obliged to give their consent. Third, consumer consent has been misused and overused by the AdTech industry for years (Bruvere & Lovic, 2021). For instance, unlike first-party cookies, third-party cookies are almost not necessary for the functioning of a website. However, the industry uses it for other purposes, including targeted advertising, and nobody takes responsibility for those cookies (Eijk et al., 2012). Additionally, consent might be given by incapacitated individuals (children), even if they lack the legal capacity, and it may cause serious damages. These problems reveal that idealizing and glorifying informed consent is not the solution, since the existing structure based on consent brings many issues, such as violation of privacy, inappropriate use of data, data and identity theft, child abuse, and so on. According to Richards and Hartzog (2019), the solution is not to find new ways to alleviate privacy concerns, but rather establish a relationship with consumers that consent is less necessary.

As one can see, the AdTech industry abuses consumers' reluctance to read privacy policies, their unawareness regarding surveillance techniques and use of personal data, and their powerlessness against the industry. Although it is almost impossible to eliminate power asymmetry, it is pretty clear that the AdTech industry and consumer relationship should be more balanced in favor of consumers. Balancing this relationship requires improving digital media literacy, unconditional transparency, and more consumer-oriented legal regulations all around the world.

Conclusion

The personal data of internet users have been collected through first-party and third-party tracking practices for over two decades with the promise of providing free content and personalized experiences on the internet. Today, the first- and third-party tracking mechanisms are embedded in every corner of our digital lives. This pervasive corporate surveillance is threatening the privacy of all people in the digital world. In this chapter, we have broadly discussed the case of online targeted advertising, a form of targeting consumers based on the data gathered with the technology of corporate surveillance. First, we presented an overview of web tracking and digital advertising from an historical perspective. Later, we explained the extensive developments in data protection regulations around the world and revealed the ongoing transformation the AdTech ecosystem has undergone to keep up with these changes. Finally, we discussed the aggressive use of personal data for targeted advertising practices through the lens of surveillance and commodification of personal information.

We wrote this chapter amid a transformation in the AdTech ecosystem towards a post-third-party cookie era. The use of third-party cookies for cross-site tracking and ad serving will soon be a thing of the past, but the future of web tracking is yet unclear. First-party data is likely to become one of the key resources for the AdTech ecosystem in the new era. While several leading AdTech actors have highlighted first-party data as a more transparent and privacy-safe option for data-driven businesses, it has the potential to cause new problems. First, the amount of first-party data the companies collect will increase in the new era, so do their responsibilities to protect personal data. The misuse of it might take privacy concerns to a new level by undermining consumers' trust. The data collectors should adopt an effective data governance program that includes a transparent data privacy policy to build trust with users and ensure compliance with data privacy standards. Another possible problem is that asymmetrical relationships might emerge in the AdTech industry due to more dependence on the infrastructures of the walled gardens. Besides the lean towards first-party data, several actors in the AdTech industry have suggested alternative approaches and technologies to third-party cookies. Since all of the proposals are still under development, it is too early to say which one(s) will be adopted by the industry. There is fierce competition to find alternative data collection methods to third-party cookies that will help ensure that the AdTech industry continues to function, and commercial considerations might once again override the data privacy concerns and transparency expectations of consumers. The digital advertising industry failed to live up to its pledges to improve transparency over data collection practices for many years. Therefore, the only way to ensure the protection of personal data is a modern legal framework.

References

Allmer, T. (2015). *Critical theory and social media: Between emancipation and commodification.* New York: Routledge.

Abbate, J. (1999). *Inventing the internet.* Cambridge, MA: The MIT Press.

Aiolfi, S., Bellini, S., & Pellegrini, D. (2021). Data-driven digital advertising: benefits and risks of online behavioral advertising. *International Journal of Retail & Distribution Management, 49*(7), 1089–1110. https://doi.org/10.1108/IJRDM-10-2020-0410

Ankerson, M. S. (2018). *Dot-com design: The rise of a usable, social, commercial web* (Vol. 15). New York: NYU Press.

Anton, A. I., Earp, J. B., & Young, J. D. (2010). How internet users' privacy concerns have evolved since 2002. *IEEE Security & Privacy, 1*(8), 21–27. doi:10.1109/MSP.2010.38

Austin, S., & Newman, N. (2015). *Attitudes to sponsored and branded content (native advertising).* Reuters Institute for the Study of Journalism, Digital News Report 2015. https://www.digitalnewsreport.org/essays/2015/attitudes-to-advertising/

Baek, T. H., & Morimoto, M. (2012). Stay away from me. *Journal of Advertising, 41*(1), 59–76. https://doi.org/10.2753/JOA0091-3367410105

Barlow, J.P. (1996). *A declaration of the independence of cyberspace*. EFF. https://www.eff.org/cyberspace-independence

Barwise, P., & Watkins, L. (2018). The evolution of digital dominance. In Martin, M. & Damian T. (Eds), *Digital dominance: The power of Google, Amazon, Facebook, and Apple* (pp. 21–49). Oxford: Oxford University Press.

Bernal, P. (2016). Data gathering, surveillance and human rights: Recasting the debate. *Journal of Cyber Policy, 1*(2), 243–264. https://doi.org/10.1080/23738871.2016.1228990

Bleier, A., & Eisenbeiss, M. (2015). Personalized online advertising effectiveness: The interplay of what, when, and where. *Marketing Science, 34*(5), 669–688. https://doi.org/10.1287/mksc.2015.0930

Bodle, R. (2016). A critical theory of advertising as surveillance: Algorithms, Big Data, and power. In Hamilton J., Bodle, R. & Korin E. (Eds), *Explorations in critical studies of advertising* (pp. 148–162). London: Routledge.

BPG & Google (2020). *Responsible marketing with first-party data*. Retrieved from https://www.thinkwithgoogle.com/intl/en-gb/marketing-strategies/data-and-measurement/first-party-data-bcg-report

Bright, L. F., & Daugherty, T. (2012). Does customization impact advertising effectiveness? An exploratory study of consumer perceptions of advertising in customized online environments. *Journal of Marketing Communications, 18*(1), 19–37. https://doi.org/10.1080/13527266.2011.620767

Bruvere, A. and Lovic, V. (2021). Rethinking informed consent in the context of Big Data. *Cambridge Journal of Science and Policies, 2*(2), 1–4. https://doi.org/10.17863/CAM.68396

Busch, O. (2016). The programmatic advertising principle. In Oliver, B. (Ed.), *Programmatic advertising* (pp. 3–15). Springer.

Cahn, A., Alfeld, S., Barford, P., & Muthukrishnan, S. (2016). *An empirical study of web cookies*. Proceedings of the 25th International Conference on World Wide Web, Montréal, Québec, Canada. https://doi.org/10.1145/2872427.2882991

Condé Nast (2018, January 8). *Condé Nast Expands Data Capabilities with the Evolution of Spire*. https://www.condenast.com/news/conde-nast-expands-data-capabilities-with-the-evolution-of-spire

Council of Europe. (1981). *Convention for the protection of individuals with regard to automatic processing of personal data*. https://rm.coe.int/1680078b37

Crain, M. (2018). The limits of transparency: Data brokers and commodification. *New Media & Society, 20*(1), 88–104. doi:10.1177/1461444816657096

Cyphers, B. (2021, March 3). *Google's FLoC is a terrible idea*. EFF. https://www.eff.org/deeplinks/2021/03/googles-floc-terrible-idea

Data & Marketing Association (2020). *The Seven-Step Ad Tech Guide*. Retrieved from https://dma.org.uk/article/the-seven-step-ad-tech-guide

Datagrail. (2020, January 28). *Consumer privacy expectations report*. https://www.datagrail.io/blog/data-privacy-day-survey

Dāvida, Z. (2020). Consumer rights and personalised advertising: Risk of exploiting consumer vulnerabilities. *Rīga Stradiņš University Faculty of Law*

Electronic Scientific Journal of Law, 1(16), 76–86. https://doi.org/10.25143/socr.16.2020.1.076-086

Earp, J. B., Antón, A. I., Aiman-Smith, L., & Stufflebeam, W. H. (2005). Examining Internet privacy policies within the context of user privacy values. *IEEE Transactions on Engineering Management, 52*(2), 227–237. doi:10.1109/TEM.2005.844927

European Network and Information Security Agency. (2012, November 14). *Privacy considerations of online behavioural tracking.* https://www.enisa.europa.eu/publications/privacy-considerations-of-online-behavioural-tracking

Flurry Analytics. (2021, May 25). *iOS 14 opt-in Rate - Weekly updates since launch.* https://www.flurry.com/blog/ios-14-5-opt-in-rate-idfa-app-tracking-transparency-weekly

Fourcade, M., & Healy, K. (2017). Seeing like a market. *Socio-Economic Review, 15*(1), 9–29. https://doi.org/10.1093/ser/mww033

Fuchs, C. (2012). The political economy of privacy on Facebook. *Television & New Media, 13*(2), 139–159. https://doi.org/10.1177/1527476411415699

GDPR Consent. (n.d.) Intersoft Consulting. Retrieved June 15, 2021, from https://gdpr-info.eu/issues/consent

Goel, V. (2021, June 24). An updated timeline for Privacy Sandbox milestones. *The Keyword, Google.* https://blog.google/products/chrome/updated-timeline-privacy-sandbox-milestones

Ham, C. D. (2017). Exploring how consumers cope with online behavioral advertising. *International Journal of Advertising, 36*(4), 632–658. https://doi.org/10.1080/02650487.2016.1239878

Interactive Advertising Bureau. (2021, March 09). *State of data 2021.* https://www.iab.com/wp-content/uploads/2021/03/IAB_Ipsos_State_Of_Data_2021-03.pdf

Janssen, M., Brous, P., Estevez, E., Barbosa, L. S., & Janowski, T. (2020). Data governance: Organizing data for trustworthy Artificial Intelligence. *Government Information Quarterly, 37*(3), 1–8. https://doi.org/10.1016/j.giq.2020.101493

Jebbit. (2019, June 19). *The state of consumer trust index.* https://www.jebbit.com/blog/the-key-to-brand-trust-providing-consumer-value-research-shows

Kim, H., & Huh, J. (2017). Perceived relevance and privacy concern regarding online behavioral advertising (OBA) and their role in consumer responses. *Journal of Current Issues & Research in Advertising, 38*(1), 92–105. https://doi.org/10.1080/10641734.2016.1233157

Kumar, V., & Gupta, S. (2016). Conceptualizing the evolution and future of advertising. *Journal of advertising, 45*(3), 302–317. https://doi.org/10.1080/00913367.2016.1199335

Mayer, J. R., & Mitchell, J. C. (2012). *Third-party web tracking: Policy and technology.* Proceedings of the 2012 IEEE Symposium on Security and Privacy, Piscataway, NJ. https://doi.org/10.1109/SP.2012.47

McDonald, A. M., & Cranor, L. F. (2010, October). *Americans' attitudes about internet behavioral advertising practices.* Proceedings of the 9th annual

ACM Workshop on Privacy in the Electronic Society, Chicago, IL. https://doi.org/10.1145/1866919.1866929

Microsoft. (2017). *Data governance for GDPR compliance: Principles, processes, and practices.* Retrieved from http://info.microsoft.com/rs/157-GQE-382/images/EN-GB-CNTNT-eBook-Security_GDPR-Data_Governance_for_GDPR_Compliance%5B1%5D.pdf

NBC News. (2019, December 27). *The history of internet tracking and the battle for privacy.* [Video]. YouTube. https://youtu.be/rKmO1nPGrVc

Negroponte, N. (1995). *Being digital.* New York: Alfred A. Knopf.

Norberg, P. A., Horne, D. R., & Horne, D. A. (2007). The privacy paradox: Personal information disclosure intentions versus behaviors. *Journal of Consumer Affairs, 41*(1), 100–126. https://doi.org/10.1111/j.1745-6606.2006.00070.x

Phelps, J. E., D'Souza, G., & Nowak, G. J. (2001). Antecedents and consequences of consumer privacy concerns: An empirical investigation. *Journal of Interactive Marketing, 15*(4), 2–17. https://doi.org/10.1002/dir.1019

Privitar. (2020, August 26). *Consumer trust and data privacy report.* https://www.privitar.com/press-releases/new-privitar-survey-reveals-business-opportunity-to-build-consumer-loyalty-through-data-privacy/

Raley, R. (2013). Dataveillance and countervailance. In Gitelman L (Ed.) *'Raw Data' is an Oxymoron* (pp. 121–145). Cambridge, MA: MIT Press.

Reese, P. (2002). *Doubleclick, Inc: A Strategic Transformation.* INSEAD Publishing. https://publishing.insead.edu/case/doubleclick-inc-a-strategic-transformation

Richards, N., & Hartzog, W. (2019). The pathologies of digital consent. *Washington University Law Review, 96*(6), 1461–1504.

Roderick, L. (2014). Discipline and power in the digital age: The case of the US consumer data broker industry. *Critical Sociology, 40*(5), 729–746. https://doi.org/10.1177/0896920513501350

Ruckenstein, M., & Granroth, J. (2020). Algorithms, advertising and the intimacy of surveillance. *Journal of Cultural Economy, 13*(1), 12–24. https://doi.org/10.1080/17530350.2019.1574866

Schneier, B. (2015). *Data and Goliath: The hidden battles to collect your data and control your world.* WW Norton & Company.

Schumann, J. H., von Wangenheim, F., & Groene, N. (2014). Targeted online advertising: Using reciprocity appeals to increase acceptance among users of free web services. *Journal of Marketing, 78*(1), 59–75. https://doi.org/10.1509/j4-m.11.0316

Sheehan, K. B., & Hoy, M. G. (1999). Flaming, complaining, abstaining: How online users respond to privacy concerns. *Journal of Advertising, 28*(3), 37–51. https://doi.org/10.1080/00913367.1999.10673588

Shoenberger, H. (2017). Targeted digital advertising and privacy. In S. Rodgers and E. Thorson, *Digital advertising: Theory and research* (pp. 300–309). London: Routledge.

Skeggs, B., & Yuill, S. (2016). Capital experimentation with person/a formation: How Facebook's monetization refigures the relationship between property, personhood and protest. *Information, Communication & Society, 19*(3), 380–396. https://doi.org/10.1080/1369118X.2015.1111403

Smit, E. G., Van Noort, G., & Voorveld, H. A. (2014). Understanding online behavioural advertising: User knowledge, privacy concerns and online coping behaviour in Europe. *Computers in Human Behavior, 32*, 15–22. http://dx.doi.org/10.1016/j.chb.2013.11.008

Tene, O., & Polenetsky, J. (2012). To track or do not track: Advancing transparency and individual control in online behavioral advertising. *Minnesota Journal of Law, Science & Technology, 13*(1), 281–357. http://dx.doi.org/10.2139/ssrn.1920505

Toubiana, V., & Verdot, V. (2011). Show me your cookie and I will tell you who you are. *arXiv preprint arXiv:1108.5864.*

Tucker, C. E. (2012). The economics of advertising and privacy. *International Journal of Industrial Organization, 30*(3), 326–329. https://doi.org/10.1016/j.ijindorg.2011.11.004

Tucker, C. E. (2014). Social networks, personalized advertising, and privacy controls. *Journal of Marketing Research, 51*(5), 546–562. https://doi.org/10.1509/jmr.10.0355

Turn, R. (1990). *Information privacy issues for the 1990s.* Proceedings of the 1990 IEEE Computer Society Symposium on Research in Security and Privacy, Oakland, CA. https://doi.org/10.1109/RISP.1990.63867

Turow, J. (2012). *The daily you: How the new advertising industry is defining your identity and your worth.* New Haven, CT: Yale University Press.

Turow, J., King, J., Hoofnagle, C. J., Bleakley, A., & Hennessy, M. (2009). Americans reject tailored advertising and three activities that enable it. https://doi.org/10.2139/ssrn.1478214

Underwood, C. (2021, April 12). Birdwatching for marketers: What Google's FLoC & FLEDGE mean for you. *Search Discovery.* https://www.searchdiscovery.com/blog/floc-and-fledge-clarity-for-marketing

United States Department of Health, Education & Welfare. (1973). *Report of the Secretary's Advisory Committee on Automated Personal Data Systems, Records, computers, and the Rights of Citizens.* https://www.justice.gov/opcl/docs/rec-com-rights.pdf

United States Government Accountability Office. (2008). *Privacy: Alternatives Exist for Enhancing Protection of Personally Identifiable Information.* https://www.gao.gov/assets/gao-08-536.pdf

Ur, B., Leon, P. G., Cranor, L. F., Shay, R., & Wang, Y. (2012). *Smart, useful, scary, creepy: Perceptions of online behavioral advertising.* Proceedings of the Eighth Symposium on Usable Privacy and Security, New York. https://doi.org/10.1145/2335356.2335362

van Dijck, J. (2014). Datafication, dataism and dataveillance: Big Data between scientific paradigm and ideology. *Surveillance & Society, 12*(2), 197–208. https://doi.org/10.24908/ss.v12i2.4776

van Eijk, N., Helberger, N., Kool, L., van der Plas, A., & van der Sloot, B. (2012). Online tracking: Questioning the power of informed consent. *Info, 14*(5), 57–73.

Warren, S. D., & Brandeis, L. D. (1890). Right to privacy. *Harvard Law Review, 4*(5), 193–220.

West, S. M. (2019). Data capitalism: Redefining the logics of surveillance and privacy. *Business & Society, 58*(1), 20–41. https://doi.org/10.1177/0007650317718185

What is considered personal data under the EU GDPR? (n.d.) GDPR.EU. Retrieved February 01, 2021, from https://gdpr.eu/eu-gdpr-personal-data

White, A. (2021, March 31). Google ends cookies and the ad industry has alternatives. *Bloomberg Technology.* https://www.bloomberg.com/news/articles/2021-03-31/google-is-ending-cookies-and-the-ad-industry-has-an-alternative

Wills, C. E., & Zeljkovic, M. (2011). A personalized approach to web privacy: Awareness, attitudes and actions. *Information Management & Computer Security, 19*(1), 53–73. https://doi.org/10.1108/09685221111115863

Xu, H., Luo, X. R., Carroll, J. M., & Rosson, M. B. (2011). The personalization privacy paradox: An exploratory study of decision making process for location-aware marketing. *Decision Support Systems, 51*(1), 42–52. https://doi.org/10.1016/j.dss.2010.11.017

Zuboff, S. (2019). *The age of surveillance capitalism: The fight for a human future at the new frontier of power: Barack Obama's books of 2019.* London: Profile Books.

Notes

1 For a detailed study of privacy in the US, see Sarah E. Igo, *The Known Citizen: A History of Privacy in Modern America* (Harvard University Press, 2018).
2 Gopher protocol was created by a team of programmers at the University of Minnesota and it was the first popular means of accessing the internet.
3 For a detailed guideline of data governance practices, see John Ladley, *Data Governance: How to Design, Deploy, and Sustain an Effective Data Governance Program* (Academic Press, 2019).
4 Australian Privacy Principles (APP) establishes the standards for the collection and handling of personal information of Australian citizens. https://www.oaic.gov.au/privacy/australian-privacy-principles
5 CPPA (Consumer Privacy Protection Act) was introduced in November 2020. It aims to establish a new private sector data privacy law, updating and replacing the existing Personal Information Protection and Electronic Documents Act (PIPEDA), which is the current Canadian federal privacy legislation for private sector organizations.
6 The Personal Data Protection Act (PDPA) is the principal personal data protection legislation in Singapore. https://www.pdpc.gov.sg
7 https://www.ozoneproject.com
8 https://www.openap.tv
9 The term "walled garden" was coined by John Malone to describe a closed platform (or ecosystem) in which all operations are controlled by the service provider. Companies such as Google, Facebook, and Amazon are usually referred to as the walled gardens of AdTech.
10 A detailed report on the adoption of data protection and privacy legislation worldwide is available on UN Conference on Trade and Development (UNCTAD)'s website. https://unctad.org/page/data-protection-and-privacy-legislation-worldwide

11 Partnership for Responsible Addressable Media (PRAM) is a collaborative cross-media initiative to develop targeted AdTech while safeguarding privacy. https://www.responsibleaddressablemedia.com
12 https://developer.chrome.com/docs/privacy-sandbox/floc/
13 https://developer.chrome.com/docs/privacy-sandbox/fledge/
14 https://github.com/WICG/turtledove/blob/main/FLEDGE.md
15 https://github.com/SWAN-community/swan
16 https://www.thetradedesk.com/us/about-us/industry-initiatives/unified-id-solution-2-0
17 According to US National Institute of Standards and Technology (NIST), a pseudonymous identifier is a meaningless but unique number that does not allow the relying party to infer anything regarding the subscriber but which does permit the relying party to associate multiple interactions with the subscriber's claimed identity. https://csrc.nist.gov/glossary/term/pseudonymous_identifier
18 Private and Anonymized Requests for Ads that Keep Efficacy and Enhance Transparency (PARAKEET) is Microsoft's proposal for the post-third-party cookie era. https://github.com/WICG/privacy-preserving-ads/blob/main/Parakeet.md

4 Smartphones, APIs & GNSS (Not GPS) Location Data

Tommy Cooke

Location data: what does that mean exactly? In the context of your smartphone, when you open Google maps, this is what you see: mailing addresses, postal codes, points of interests, and Global Positioning System (GPS) coordinates. The former most are perhaps the least obvious as such, and perhaps that is because they are discernible from the latter as human-readable information. So, GPS coordinates seem to stand apart. They can be displayed and read when we tap and hold our fingertip in a navigation app. They are presented to us as a measurement, which is significant to users because they are done so within the context that they are presented – with human-readable information. Our device, it seems, reminds us that it is as much a communication technology as it is a powerful scientific instrument capable of exacting our whereabouts – almost anywhere in the world – within a radius no larger than the width of the street. Indeed, smartphone location accuracy is increasing. But it is far more accurate than the device suggests through Google Maps, and I argue that the device's hidden accuracy is far more compromising to our location privacy than meets the eye. This chapter explores the world of raw location measurements and the internal and cloud-based algorithms responsible for engineering not only an invasively granular-level location tracking that users never see, but also responsible for granting entire industries, governments, and burgeoning marketplaces access to discrete highly detailed location data that is far more sensitive than users are ever able to easily and conveniently access within their own device. This chapter begins by teasing apart the differences between what users, the media, politicians, and academics alike tend to believe are smartphone location data (GPS coordinates) against some of the raw measurements that smartphone navigation satellite receivers *actually* produce: global navigation satellite system (GNSS) raw measurements. After understanding the difference between the two, the chapter briefly discusses why

DOI: 10.4324/9781003173335-4

manufacturers have a stake in perpetuating popular conflation of the former with the latter. This is precisely because GNSS raw measurements and the algorithms in the smartphone's operating system responsible for collecting, calculating, and circulating them are designed as a technoscientific sandbox – an invitation for engineers, software designers, and analytics developers around the globe to experiment in ways that make smartphones more accurate than they are capable of determining on their own, but also in ways that radically undermine how we as critical thinkers engage about the concept and the future of location privacy itself.[1]

GPS coordinates: an overview

Prior to understanding how location privacy is collapsing, it is important to have a high-level sense of the technology responsible for location tracking. The first thing that tends to come to mind in the smartphone privacy debate and discourse is "GPS". While it is true that GPS is relevant to smartphones today, it is no longer the sole technology responsible for determining location via navigation satellites. This comes with an important caveat: smartphones certainly rely upon multiple methods for determining location and not merely via navigation satellites. Cellular towers and Wi-Fi triangulation often come to mind here. While these other methods are certainly important, they are not the focus here. This section first focuses on GPS technology on smartphones, and then shifts to something more encompassing and more flexible than GPS: GNSS technology, which replaced GPS on smartphones nearly a decade ago. Nevertheless, I digress. Let us begin with some background discussion on GPS so that we can then more properly understand how smartphones actually determine location via navigation satellites.

GPS did not begin in smartphones, but nor is its origin simply a handheld technology. GPS was launched in the early 1970s by the US Department of Defense as a technological network comprised of navigation satellites, handheld receivers, and ground stations. As a technological network, GPS was designed as a solution to imprecise weapon delivery and to overcome challenges with tracking assets such as special operators and military vehicles around the globe (Pace et al., 1995). The initial launch of the GPS system involved 24 satellites, which did not become available for public use until 1995. The context for initiating public usage of GPS was initially public safety. Soon thereafter, GPS receivers began appearing inside cellular phones as both standalone and integrated chipsets. The first smartphone of its kind was called *Esc!*, which was produced by Benefon that was marketed as a safety device (Sarkola, 2000). Approximately six years later, GPS receivers began appearing for non-safety-related purposes and on a much larger manufacturing scale. While the majority of those initial phone sales were within the European markets, they quickly spread to North American markets. In effect, phones across both continents had (a) navigation satellite receivers that could (b) intercept signals transmitted by GPS satellites.

And yet, the GPS satellite constellation was not the only satellite constellation available for public and military use at the time. The GLONASS constellation, short for "Global Navigation Satellite System," was developed by the Soviet Union in 1976 to compete with GPS. A few years after the US made GPS available for civilian use, the Russian Federation made a similar move by making GLONASS available for public use in 2001. Phones manufactured for use in Russia had receiver technology that was different from GPS receiver technology; phones sold in Russian markets could intercept GLONASS navigation satellite signals, while phones sold in European and American markets were designed to intercept GPS navigation satellite signals. For a time, phones could *not* intercept navigation satellite signals from different navigation satellite constellations. Then came ZTE's MTS 945, the first device that could intercept *both* GPS and GLONASS signals. The MTS 945 did not use a GPS receiver. It used something a bit different, something that is simply referred to within industry as a GNSS receiver. It functions similarly to a GPS receiver, except that it is capable of intercepting navigation satellite signals from more than one satellite constellation.

Despite this significant change in the technology, it is important to note that some of the earliest discourse on phone-driven navigation satellite technology retained the label of GPS without signaling the fact that GNSS receivers were entirely replacing GPS receivers on virtually all phones worldwide by the early 2010s – not merely in Russia. Take, for example, some early 2010 news headlines surrounding the supposed nexus of national security and navigation satellite receiver proliferation. The headline reads, "Russian GPS using U.S. Soil Stirs Spy Fears" (Schmidt and Schmitt, 2013). Here is another: "Russia has not allowed the U.S. to construct GPS monitor stations in Russia" (McKinnis, 2013). And another: "owning GPS has a number of advantages, but the first and foremost is that global military and commercial users depend on this service of the U.S. government" (Crichton and Tabatabai, 2018). This tendency to misrepresent the technology was echoed in government security discourse as well; a former Russian

Deputy Prime Minister launched an investigation into GPS operations in Russia, stating "we already receive the GPS signal [in Russia].
The question arises how the U.S. navigation system GPS operates in
Russia" (TASS Russian News Agency, 2013). This recursive invocation of the abbreviation "GPS" within both media and government
discourse was and remains a source of knowledge about the capabilities of "Big Brother," as it were, particularly throughout the rapidly
emerging public and popular discourses on location privacy beginning in the 2010s – a time where we see similar public and popular
tendencies to invoke "GPS" as a technological catchall. "The three
most important keys to retail success are also the most important ones
to your privacy in the 21st century," Tynan writes for *Computer World*
magazine in 2010. "Which is why you should be keeping a watchful eye
on all those big corporations that keeping a watchful eye on you… All
of these companies have recently added (or are on the verge of adding)
location-centric services." Google, Twitter, Apple, Facebook, Four-
Square, and the mobile devices that hosted their apps such as iPhones
and Androids were feared for the ways in which precise, real-time location of their users could be offloaded for profit and national security
purposes. As handheld devices around the globe were increasingly
incorporating GPS capabilities, Haggerty and Ericsson (2003) were
theorizing surveillance as a force driven by the coalescing of interests
between public and private sector actors for mutual benefit. GPS was
a primary example of what they meant.

Alas, surveillance and privacy scholarship continued incorrectly
reifying GPS as a catchall technological concept for thinking about,
with, and through navigation satellite system capabilities on phones.
Consider the definitions of personal information provided by otherwise contrasting institutions in terms of their social utility, such as the
Office of the Privacy Commissioner of Canada (OPC) and Google,
Inc. The former defines personal information, vis-à-vis the Personal
Information Protection and Electronics Documents Act (2005) as "information about an identifiable individual," which includes "tracking
information collected from a Global Positioning System (GPS)" (OPC,
2013). The latter defines personal information rather similarly as "information that could be used on its own to directly identify, contact,
or precisely locate an individual. This includes… precise locations
(such as GPS coordinates…)" (Google Analytics Help, 2021). Note the
explicit invocation of GPS. Whether national security discourse, public and popular debate on location privacy, or definitions of personal
information invoked by even the most virtually opposed of actors,
what each iteration has in common is constraining the ontology of

phone-based satellite navigation technology. By the early 2010s, most every "smart" phone in the planet was using GNSS technology, not GPS technology. The shift first began with Qualcomm, who manufactured the Snapdragon MSM7x30 (Wilson, 2011) – a chipset with a GNSS receiver. While technical literature (such as user manuals, grey papers, and design and technical specification documents within automotive navigation, air navigation, maritime navigation, automated machine navigation, and spacecraft engineering) differentiated GNSS from GPS quite explicitly for many decades, the trend failed to catch on within the public sphere. Even though the term "GNSS" appeared frequently in the UN Office for Outer Space Affairs (UNOOSA) consumer market trend reports since well before 2010 as well as in similar literature produced by the EU's Global Navigation Satellite Systems Agency (EGNSSA), the differentiation failed to catch on elsewhere. Failures to differentiate between the two technologies when talking about smartphones normalized the technological imagination of the public, the media, politicians, policy makers and so forth. It also constrains how their technological imagination thinks about smartphone *location data* as well.

GPS versus GNSS

If you were to think about GPS-related location data, what would come to mind? If searched online, for example, you would encounter something that looks like *coordinates*: minutes, degrees, and seconds representing latitude and longitude (e.g., 41°24'12.2"N, 2°10'26.5"E) or more popularly reformatted on smartphone apps such as Google Maps in decimal degrees (e.g., 41.403389, 2.174028). If you were to open Google Maps or download your location history, these are the kind of "location data" you would indeed find. For all intents and purposes, we can refer to them as GPS data. However, GPS data are not what smartphone navigation satellite chipsets produce. This is largely due to how smartphones interact with the signals that navigation satellites transmit. This is an important process that is often misunderstood as it is rather technically complicated, but it is an important process to – at the very least – attempt to understand if only from a high level.

The way that smartphone GNSS receivers assist the device in determining its location is by calculating and measuring content residing within the signal itself. This process does not output GPS coordinates, as it were. Rather, it first produces calculations of *delay in time*.[1] This is because navigation satellites transmit the time found in its onboard atomic clock. Approximately twice a day, a navigation satellite will generally pass overheard. Despite the speed of the signal being approximately 180,000 mph (which is close to the speed of light), there is a *delay* between the time that the satellite transmits the time in the signal it beams toward the planet and the time that the smartphone's GNSS receiver detects that same signal. It is precisely the difference in the transmission and the receivable time that the GNSS receiver uses to begin calculating the device's location. However, one signal from one satellite does not provide enough data to determine where the device geographically resides. This is because the device is only calculating time differences between two objects, thus creating a linear measurement. As such, it is not self-evidently three-dimensional. Hence the need for all GNSS receivers to intercept signals from at least three navigation satellites. Consider, for example, how a navigation satellite may be approximately 12,000 miles away as it passes overhead. Now consider how its orbit unfolds in three-dimensions: its heading and altitude unfold, much like an aircraft, along *x, y,* and *z* axes. Accordingly, it is helpful for us to consider that the space between the satellite and the surface of the planet must be measured in three-dimensions as well. Signals do not transmit in two, but three-dimensions. If a satellite transmits a signal from 12,000 miles away, that signal will cover at least 12,000 miles of horizontal geography on the planet's surface as well. You might then imagine that a smartphone cannot calculate its geographical location by calculating time delays emanating from one source. Now consider the same smartphone simultaneously calculating time delays transmitted from three navigation satellites – all at different orbit altitudes, different trajectories, potentially different atomic clock times, different transmission and receipt times, and as such, different distances from the device itself. Each satellite transmits a signal with unique characteristics, but in ways that *overlap* in three-dimensions. The device's calculation of these time delay differences from three or more satellites is what allows it to determine where it is, geographically speaking, within the area of geospatial overlap caused by intersecting signal transmissions. Around the space of the smartphone, there will be an approximate 5 meter to 10 meter space where more than three unique navigation satellite signals overlap. It is within this space that the smartphone believes itself to exist. This is what is referred to as *trilateration.* What is as important to understand as the aforementioned is how this process that takes place in the GNSS receiver documents the calculations it produces. With the focal point of trilateration is indeed calculating delay in time, the process also outputs numerous variables in the form of one of two data sentences. One of those is called the National Marine Electronics Association (NMEA) 0183 – a data format worthy of focus and critique indeed, but which is beyond the scope of this chapter.[2] The other format produced – the focus of this paper – is called *GNSS Raw Measurement*.[3] I have extracted an example of one of these sentences from ongoing research that began at Queen's University's Surveillance Studies Centre in the fall of 2020:

> Raw,   169806580,227724071000000,-1238885499373429248,0.0,82.0571294752881,   2.4674019091539217,16.124495093118234,54,14,0.0, 207,61605369492321,31,23.3,655.6437377929688,0.9399999976158142,0,0.0,0.0,0,3,0.0

This sample data string can be read, in a sense, by understanding its structure. The first word, "raw," indicates that we are indeed encountering raw GNSS data. Between each "," are numbers, each with a different value. Some of these numbers are calculations, some are measurements, and others are approximations. Each value serves a different technoscientific purpose, depending upon the needs and requirements of the "calculator" that these data are given to. In this case, it is the smartphone's operating system, which then calculates the variables provided within the data string to produce information such as latitude, longitude, velocity, distance traveled, direction of travel, and so on. This particular string is absent of certain fields, as evidenced by the consecutive appearance of commas without data between them. The reason is that this raw GNSS data string is a sample from the data tracking experiment my team and I conducted in late 2019. Our test smartphone was not moving and the recording length was not significant. In most circumstances, the majority – if not all – of these fields will contain data, a list of which is provided below (see Table 4.1).

The table provides a general sense of some, but not all, of the data variables a smartphone's GNSS receiver outputs. Notice that the chipset does *not* simply produce "GPS data" as it were. There are no latitude and longitude coordinates here. The process of determining the device's location is indeed tremendously facilitated by processes provided by the chipset, but things become considerably more complicated within the smartphone *before* any such coordinates are produced. This layer of complication resides in the device's Java Application Programming Interface (API) Framework, and it is here that the paper's location privacy concerns begin to unfold.

GNSS data and Google Android's location APIs

The API is a section of the operating system that allows applications to interact with other sections of the operating system. It can be thought

Table 4.1 GNSS Raw Measurement Variables

Gnss Clock	
TimeNanos	GNSS Receiver hardware clock value
TimeUncertaintyNano	Uncertainty of above value
FullBiasNanos	Difference between received clock and "true" time since 0000Z, 6 January 1980
DriftNanosPerSecond	Receiver clock's drift
DriftUncertaintyNanosPerSecond	Uncertainty of above value
HardwareClockDiscontinuityCount	Count of hardware clock discontinuities
Gnss Measurement	
Svid	Satellite ID
ConstellationType	BeiDou, Galileo, GLONASS, GPS, QZAA, SBAS
TimeOffsetNanos	Time offset if measurements are synchronous
State	Sync state (code lock, bit sync, frame sync, etc.)
ReceivedSvTimeNanos	Received satellite time, at the measurement time
ReceivedSvTimeUncertaintyNanos	Error estimate of above value
Cn0DbHz	Carrier-to-noise density ratio
PseudorangeRateMetersPerSecond	Pseudorange rate (Doppler)
PseudorangeRateUncertaintyMetersPerSecond	Error estimate of above value
AccumulatedDeltaRangeMeters	Accumulated delta range (carrier phase)
AccumulatedDeltaRangeUncertaintyMeters	Error estimate of above value
AccumulatedDeltaRangeState	Valid, Cycle slip or Loss-of-lock/Reset
CarrierFrequencyHz	Carrier frequency of the tracked signal
AgcDb	Automatic Gain Control level

of as an intermediary that accepts, facilitates, and executes requests on behalf of an application that requires a measurement, access to a sensor, entries from a library, or data.[4] In public talks, I often describe APIs in smartphones as both *data brokers* and *data envoys*: the former in the sense that APIs are used to allow one piece of software to make requests to access important functions, tasks, algorithms, or data. But an API can also refer to the latter, in the sense that they are official representatives of an operating system or platform. The terms are useful for thinking critically about APIs, particularly their politics: how and whether an application may or may not receive and request the processes and data it requires depends upon the agency of the API. Because an API represents a specific software system, it is governed by that software system via rules and limitations within which the API can and cannot operate. While these rules and limitations are not necessarily explicitly declared in a self-evident way, it is helpful to keep in mind that these rules and limitations reflect the manufacturer's business strategy. At the level of code, APIs are given to application developers as instructions that are not only cut and paste into the architecture of their app. The API can also be highly customized so as to efficiently carry out complex functions. The extent to which APIs function as such is thus only limited by how a manufacturer perceives what tasks, data types, and areas of access that an app developer desires. We might consider then how the evolution of a software system is a very social and not merely a technical process. As I will discuss in more detail below, the location APIs in a Google Android device have considerably matured to reflect specific industrial desires for increasingly more and more sensitive types of smartphone location measurements. The matter of how and whether access to these measurements is a necessity as opposed to a privilege, as well as the question of what is done with the content an API provides, is precisely why APIs are most certainly political technologies, particularly when it comes to location privacy.

Because my research on the politics of smartphone location data focuses on Google Android devices, I will now focus on them in more detail here. The Java API Framework in Android devices has a library of location-specific processes. Within the app development guideline Google publishes online, this library is referred to as the "Android. Location" API directory. It is often also more simply referred to as "Google Location Services." This directory consists of functions that allow an app to request, access, handle, calculate, derive, smooth, copy, and circulate location data. To clarify, apps do not determine the device's location on their own – location APIs perform this function on their behalf. The way in which this unfolds is through two subtypes of APIs: classes and interfaces. The former refers to a programming language process that assists a developer to create software "objects," which are, generally speaking, a data output or product. Classes are blueprints for creating these objects in different ways, which assists in defining how data-related functions unfold. Classes contain what are called "methods" or blocks of code that are executed when called upon by an app. They can be individualized and isolated as such, but are more commonly bundled to output an object that an app desires. Interfaces can allow developers to group together different classes and define a higher-level set of behaviors that guide how specific classes might work together. The difference between the two is less important for us as nonexperts as is what their abundance means to interacting with location data. The primary takeaway here is recognizing that location data-related interfaces and classes are created by Google and made available to developers so that they can combine and orchestrate different groups of algorithms to achieve specific data goal-driven outcomes.

At the time of writing this chapter, the "Android.Location" API consists of five interfaces and 22 classes. The combined total of methods that can be used to act upon location data by an app is approximately 334. For the sake of simplicity, the API directory can be hierarchically visualized in this way:

⇨ Android (Operating System)
⇨ Java API Framework
⇨ Location.Android (directory)
⇨ Interfaces (five in total)
⇨ Classes (twenty-two in total)
⇨ Methods (three hundred and thirty-four in total)

Of particular concern to this chapter is a specific class called "GNS-SMeasurement," which is visualized below. This class is the primary API that allows an app to access the raw GNSS measurement data sentence observed earlier in the chapter. Notice within the table that the number and names of each individual method corresponds closely to the comma-separated data fields depicted by the GNSS raw measurement data sentence seen in Table 1. There are 40 methods in total within the GNSSMeasurement class, which provides an app developer (and subsequently, their app) novel ways of accessing the approximately 20 individual data variables found within the GNSS raw measurement data string itself:

⇨ Location.Android (directory)
⇨ GNSSMeasurement Class
⇨ describeContents()
⇨ getAccumulatedDeltaRangeMeters()
⇨ getAccumulatedDeltaRangeState()
⇨ getAccumulatedDeltaRangeUncertaintyMeters()
⇨ getAutomaticGainControlLevelDb()
⇨ getBasebandCn0DbHz()
⇨ getCarrierCycles()
⇨ getCarrierFrequencyHz()
⇨ getCarrierPhase()

⇨ getCarrierPhaseUncertainty()
⇨ getCn0DbHz()
⇨ getCodeType()
⇨ getConstellationType()
⇨ getFullInterSignalBiasNanos()
⇨ getFullInterSignalBiasUncertaintyNanos()
⇨ getMultipathIndicator()
⇨ getPseudorangeRateMetersPerSecond()
⇨ getPseudorangeRateUncertaintyMetersPerSecond()
⇨ getReceivedSvTimeNanos()
⇨ getReceivedSvTimeUncertaintyNanos()
⇨ getSatelliteInterSignalBiasNanos()
⇨ getSatelliteInterSignalBiasUncertaintyNanos()
⇨ getSnrInDb()
⇨ getState()
⇨ getSvid()
⇨ getTimeOffsetNanos()
⇨ hasAutomaticGainControlLeveldB()
⇨ hasBasebandCn0DbHz()
⇨ hasCarrierCycles()
⇨ hasCarrierFrequencyHz()
⇨ hasCarrierPhase()
⇨ hasCarrierPhaseUncertainty()
⇨ hasCodeType()
⇨ hasFullIntegerSignalBiasNanos()
⇨ hasFullIntegerSignalBiasUncertaintyNanos()
⇨ hasSnrInDb()
⇨ toString()
⇨ writeToParcel()

The number of methods is overwhelming to read for both experts and nonexperts, and it is only a fraction of the number of different methods that an app can draw upon. What makes this class particularly important is not merely that it is designed to isolate many of the data variables found between the commas of the data sentence and return them to an app; Google describes this class to app developers as both a retrieval tool for raw measurements *but also computer location information*. For example, by combining the getPseudorangeRateMetersPerSecond() method with getSvid() and getConstellationType() inside of the code of an app, app developers effectively program their app to retrieve a new data output that provides specific information about the device. In this example's context, the API would provide the app the first semblance of what we might consider as location information, indicating in this case the rate of travel (in meters per second) of a specific satellite, within a specified satellite constellation (e.g., GLONASS, GALILEO, BEIDOU, GPS, et al.). While the range of possibilities that a Google Android device's APIs presents for an app developer suggests flexibility, precision, creativity, and control over location data, the point here is that how and where GNSS raw measurements are treated in the process is anything but linear and centralized. As importantly, we also recognize that none of the outputs described here are presented in the form of GPS coordinates. These data are *also* location data, but are completely *different* from what a user sees when inquiring about their "location data" on their device. As you can see, the number of possibilities for apps to create new data outputs or location information is exponential. In what Shoshana Zuboff recently articulated as the *asymmetry* of data – whereby the difference between what users see (and thus engage, understand, and relate to as a representation of data itself) and what third-parties collect – is dangerously different. I use the word dangerous very deliberately here, precisely because it is the absence of knowledge about what happens with the undercurrent of nonmainstream, non-GPS coordinate location data that is currently fueling the development of new location accuracy algorithms, ones that I argue are actively playing a role in the collapse of smartphone-based location privacy.

GNSS, location APIs, and precision point positioning: an emerging horizon of concern

Earlier in the chapter, I made a case regarding the way in which APIs can be thought of as political technologies. This is not only observable through the exponentially endless ways in which they collect and create new location data/information for apps in ways that users almost never see. Their politics can also be explained historically in the context of their development by Google for Android devices. One of the most significant yet virtually undiscussed years for the evolution of location data as a social problem was 2016: the year that Google announced for the very first time that GNSS raw measurements would be made available to industry (Lei et al., 2021). While it was indeed true that these measurements have always been produced by GNSS chipsets in smartphones since their implementation in the early 2010s, the chipset was essentially a black box; the data these chipsets output were provided directly to the operating system alone. But in 2016, Google created new location APIs that would encourage not merely app developers but engineers and scientists to build and use the APIs – whether in the form of apps or other software – to pull GNSS raw measurements from smartphones. The announcement by Google should not be left undisturbed as something of a "natural step" in the evolution of the Android smartphone. The announcement was an invitation:

> "This is groundbreaking", said Steve Malkos, a technical program manager at Google. "It is the first time in history that a mobile application will have access to the raw GPS measurements. This is beneficial to many, but especially the phone makers, because they can use these measurements to help them in their performance testing. And if you ever had a bright idea on how to use GPS measurements, now's your time to shine"
>
> (Malkos, 2016)

Interestingly enough, a technical manager at Google conflated GPS with GNSS when describing GNSS measurements. I digress because doing so many have been intentional as a strategy for attempting to capture the curiosity of Android "users." Consider a response to Google's announcement, which was posted by the EU Agency for the Space Programme (EUSPA): "With the release of Android 7 (Nougat) in 2016, Google made GNSS raw measurements available to smartphone users, allowing them to improve their positioning accuracy." The response was provided via Market Development Innovation Officer Martin Sunkevic of the EGNSS Agency. He further stated that:

> in the area of research and development, the measurements could be used to test hardware and software solutions for new algorithms, such as for modelling the ionosphere or troposphere. But the benefits to users do not stop there. Access to raw measurements also means that developers can now use advanced positioning techniques to create solutions that are currently only available in professional receivers.

Between the two statements, there appears to be something of a seemingly interchangeable invocation of "user" with "developers." Malkos and Sunkevic may be envisioning a distant world where casual smartphone users build software to retrieve nanosecond-level measurements of satellite signals for pertinent purposes. Given that causal users are only socialized into their location data vis-à-vis "GPS coordinates," it may be fairer to assume here that Malkos and Sunkevic mean something quite different when they share their excitement about who can access these measurements and why they might want to in the first place. To the contrary, Malkos and Sunkevic are referring to users with a specific set of interests, skillsets, and professional preoccupations. These may not necessarily be app developers themselves, but rather industry-specific engineers, scientists, and software developers who have a stake in wanting to technically improve upon the location capabilities of smartphones themselves.

One such area of experts who have an interest and stake in accessing these measurements are the geoscientists – researchers in the area of planetary natural science. The field is acutely interested in atmospheric phenomena, events that interfere with electronic signals due to the ways in which they affect GNSS performance. Recalling that a smartphone determines a device's location vis-à-vis navigation satellite signals by calculating the *delay* in signal transmission and receivable time, considerable geoscientific research is directed toward GNSS-equipped technologies. Numerous scholarly publications with specific industrial applications and stakes in navigation satellite-aided technology are invested in promoting "user" awareness of how electromagnetic waves within the ionosphere interfere with satellite signal quality (Taoufiq et al., 2018). Since the 2010s, the geosciences laid new intellectual terrain for identifying and translating the sources of signal loss, disruption, and degradation as they result in nature (Adekunle, 2014) and through human interference catalyzed by dense urban architectural design (Andrianarison et al., 2018). Throughout the decade, geoscientific research also galvanized technoscientific consensus about the limitations of smartphones themselves (Lohan, 2011; Lamontagne, 2012; Mollaiyan et al., 2013; Ma et al., 2019). This is a considerably important factor for thinking critically about what was at stake when Google "opened access" to GNSS raw measurements in Android devices. "Low-power" and "consumer-grade" electronics are common terms among a body of research that established industry-wide knowledge about not what smartphones can do in terms of determining their own location, but rather what they *cannot* do on their own terms. In essence, they declared the devices as fraught with technical problems that required technical interventions.

By the mid-2010s, the geosciences and Google were at a crossroads. Research surrounding the limitations of GNSS devices is well known. There was indeed a transfer of knowledge about the known limits of smartphones as navigation satellite-capable devices, one which initially emerged through independent geoscientific study of independent, high-powered, handheld navigation receivers. But that knowledge transfer required an intermediary, which happened to be Google.

By "opening access" to GNSS raw measurements in 2016, the geosciences moved directly toward smartphones. I am intentionally stylizing "opening access" to draw consideration to the fact that Google did not simply, as GPS World Magazine initially said (Malkos, 2016), open a door to industry. Google built the door, along with the tools required to walk through it and retrieve what was on the other side. Recall from earlier that GNSS raw measurement access on Android devices arrived with Nougat version 7.0 of the Android operating system. Prior to Nougat was Marshmallow, which was pushed to Android devices on 2 October 2015 before being replaced by its successor a little less than a year later, on 22 August 2016. Marshmallow operated on API level 23 and its successor on API level 24. API level refers to an integer value that uniquely represents the version or "level" of a smartphone operating system's framework revision (Brandi, 2019). Simply, it is an iteration of the Java component of an operating system that is responsible for offering APIs. It is standard practice within the smartphone manufacturing industry for API levels to increase at each major operating system release. But they are not synchronous with the level of the operating system itself.

For example, Marshmallow was operating system version 7, but released at API level 23. This means that numerous preceding operating system versions contained multiple API framework updates. While the detail may seem insignificant, it is particularly helpful to us as critical thinkers for two reasons. First, operating system versions are advertised with attractive names. From Cupcake and Donut to Honeycomb and Jelly Bean, users are socialized by manufacturers into operating systems in ways that are palatable and meaningful in terms of their supposed usage experience. Each major version often arrives with significant changes to not only performance and accessibility, but with visual and auditory aesthetic changes to colors and sounds – a mechanism that, as I have argued in the past (Cooke, 2020), normalizes system updates in ways that depoliticize substantive and critical changes to the most important levels of a device's operating system architecture. For example, Google's release of version 10 of the Android operating system in 2020 promoted an entirely overhauled visual experience with new app open and close visualizations, new swipe animations, and the introduction of an edge-of-screen swipe feature that would allow users to quickly navigate backwards. The version delivered "dark mode" as well. Meanwhile, Google stopped providing crucial security updates to devices not using version 10, reported the UK-based consumer watchdog *Which?* (2020). Google did not inform over a billion users worldwide that they stopped providing patches to known security vulnerabilities for users of version 9. While Google was focused on improving upon an API that retrieved depth information from cameras for version 10, they stopped supporting users of version 9. But for users who did update, the Associated Press investigated and discovered in 2018 that Google's Android operating system indefinitely collected user location data regardless of whether or not Location Services was deactivated (Nakashima, 2018). Two years later, even Google's own senior engineers remain confused about how and under what conditions Android devices are collecting and transmitting location data to Google (Lopatto, 2020). What a user sees and experiences does not entirely reflect the changes made in the operating system across versions and API level revisions, and those changes can catalyze considerable implications and risky industrial developments that will affect users in one way or another.

I digress and return to my initial concern with the API level of Marshmallow, which was 23. In 2015, prior to Google's "opening access" to GNSS raw measurements, it is important to note here that none of the APIs researcher, app developer, or data scientist would require to access them existed. While general GPS-related coordinate and measurement data could be accessed through the GpsSatellite and GpsStatus location API classes, GNSS raw measurements were not accessible until 2016 – when Google announced industrial access to them. In August of that year, Android Nougat arrived. It was advertised as displaying multiple screens at once, notification replies, and even a "Doze" power-saving mode that supposedly restricted device functionality when the device's screen was powered off. What was not advertised to "users" was that Google also created 17 new location API classes that gave researchers, scientists, app developers, and private sector companies hundreds of new methods and functions for accessing and retrieving GNSS raw measurements. So long as an installed app consisted of these new APIs, any actor on the planet could pull these measurements from a user's device in real time. What this access means for location privacy, especially in terms of what it fuels in terms of algorithmic development, has tremendous consequences on the future of location privacy.

Since Google created the tools needed for industrial actors and the geosciences to access GNSS raw measurements, there has been an explosion in new research targeted at Android smartphones to develop novel algorithms, particularly algorithms that function *outside* and not *inside* the device. By "algorithms," what I mean here are the preferred software technologies through which both manufacturers and geoscientists construct "solutions" within the context of location

tracking. More specifically, I refer to automated processes that introduce additional information to aid the smartphone in reducing location calculation errors that are believed to provide "better accuracy
estimation, navigation robustness and an additional layer of security"
(EGNSSA, 2017). For example, most smartphones that process location through navigation satellites utilize an architecture within the
device called A-GNSS: "A" standing for "assisted." A-GNSS relies on
a Wi-Fi and cellular-based Internet connection to communicate with
an external server that provides estimations of the smartphone's position. It also provides calibration assistance for hardware sensors and
satellite clock correction and ionospheric modeling information (Van
Diggelen, 2009). The A-GNSS server remotely *predicts* navigation satellite behavior and sends this data back to the smartphone to assist the
device in not merely determining its own location, but improving upon
the device's location accuracy.

More concerning to the purposes of this chapter is an algorithmic
approach embodied in what is more generally referred to within the
navigation satellite systems technical community as PPP. This approach utilizes predictive algorithms to refine smartphone location
accuracy demonstrating success in determining device location within
spaces much smaller than the average 5–10-meter radii that smartphones are generally capable of determining on their own. PPP focuses specifically on data cultivated within GNSS raw measurements,
specifically the "carrier phase frequency" variable, which refers to the
"up" and "down" oscillatory movement of a signal through space.
By measuring the physical width of a signal's peak and valley as it
oscillates, PPP algorithms executed in a remote server extract these
variables directly from the smartphone's GNSS chipset via Google
Android's Location Services' APIs. Once the variables are extracted
to the server, they are calculated along with predictive models of ionospheric weather patterns. The output of this process is a string of
refined smartphone location data that are sent back to the device as
real-time updates regarding the device's location. While the PPP has
existed since the mid-1990s (Bisnath et al., 2018), recent developments
are worth monitoring in terms of what they mean to the future of location privacy on smartphones. As Richard Langley and Sunil Bisnath (Canadian Professors of Geomatics Engineering) celebrated in
an article called "Precise Point Positioning: A Power Technique with a
Promising Future" in *GPS World Magazine*:

> as the impetus for low-cost, precise positioning and navigation
> for autonomous and semi-autonomous platforms... continues to

grow, there is interest in processing such low-cost data with PPP algorithms. For example, it has [also] been shown that [similar] smartphone data can be processed with the PPP approach... There are now a number of low-cost, dual-frequency, multi-constellation products on the market, with additional such products as well as smartphone chips coming soon.

Langley and Bisnath foreshadowed PPP's uptake rather precisely. Over 1,230 articles have been published in the past decade investigating the potentials and limitations of PPP as a solution for navigation satellite-based technologies. Three significant articles have been published on *GPS World* specifically about the usage of PPP on smartphones,[6] two of which reflect upon the availability of Google Android's APIs that first made access to raw GNSS measurements on their devices available in the summer of 2016. Since that summer, 412 academic articles have been published on the usage of PPP to increase location accuracy capabilities of Google Android smartphones.

Reminiscent of Lake's (2017) potent reminder of the ontological politics of hyperindividualism, extracting and isolating data from the original context within which they are created imbues that data with an entirely new agency and meaning for users. To remove and intensely focus on data divorced from their origin is to necessarily ontologize them as building blocks for industrial development. Recalling that GNSS raw measurements have existed on smartphones for nearly six years prior to them being utilized by industry, it is important to take into account what it means to the user when they are rather suddenly situated in a place where they are immediately ascribed new meanings – ones that are completely devoid of an everyday user's awareness and understanding. Without awareness and understanding is the absence of public discussion, debate, and ultimately discourse on GNSS raw measurements' usage to fuel industrial development, equating in the simultaneous lack of public awareness about potential implications of wide scale, globally reaching, unprecedented data uptake and usage. While Lake reminds us that these absences "eviscerate[s] the possibility of collective resistance," they also do something as alarming: foster the foundation required to decentralize location processing and raw location data while placing it into the hands of private sector actors who collaborate with government. Indeed, what is at stake with PPP is the way it fundamentally recasts the function of the smartphone itself in terms of determining a user's location. Not only does PPP remove location data that are far more sensitive and high resolution than the 'GPS coordinates' that users tend to see, these data are stored elsewhere before they are transformed into new location updates that are sent *back* to the device. While PPP may be heralded throughout industry and the geosciences as a solution to the technical problem of low-powered, consumer-grade electronics that struggle to determine their location with any sense of accuracy in sub-5-to-7-meter radii, PPP assumes that agency on behalf of the user's device. This decentralization and supplanting of device autonomy raises important questions about how and whether Location Services on Android devices will have any relevance in the future. In the face of tremendous confusion in 2021 about how and whether they work at all, what does it mean for users if the lowest but most detailed level of location measurements is exported beyond their control? In what ways do location updates, created externally, implicate a system's role in a user's ability to relate to and navigate their geographical surroundings? As importantly, what are the sociopolitical ramifications of engineering accuracy at unprecedented levels?

This lattermost question is the most vital to address for privacy scholars moving forward. This is because the application of PPP is quickly rearticulating how we think about the geophysical space within which a device can be known to exist. PPP WizLite is an Android-based app developed by an entrepreneurial French-based digital services development and advisory company that specializes in developing surveillance, command, data intelligence, simulation cybersecurity, and tactical communication systems. The app was developed approximately five years ago, and in 2017 won the European Space Navigation Award for achieving geolocation accuracy in smartphones under 1 meter. The app has been promoted by Google as the most accurate device location tracking app available. PPP WizLite builds upon a preexisting system developed by the French space agency, the Centre national d'études spatiales, called the PPP-Wizard Project. It was originally designed as part of the agency's space orbit determination service. It uses algorithms to calculate orbit and clock data from within Russian and American satellites and transmit that data to users connected to the system. Users are provided with what is called "PPP Monitoring" that assists in calculating the received data. The C-S Group found a way to combine GNSS raw measurements produced by Android smartphone's navigation satellite technology with the French space agency's tracking solution system, PPP-Wizard. At the time the group received the award in Hesse, Germany, in 2017, they had already predicted that centimeter-level device tracking solutions will be possible within a few years.

GNSS industrial development and (the demise) smartphone location privacy

PPP Wizlite is not simply a smartphone tracking solution. It needs to be situated in a more critical sociopolitical context, especially if we are to understand its implications for location privacy in the future. First, the app weds automated system processes meant for military and government asset tracking with civilian smartphone architecture. While some readers may object to the notion that an app can change an operating system – which it most certainly cannot – we must remember that it was Google in 2016 that paved the way for interoperability between government, industry, and civilian mobile technology. By creating numerous location APIs specifically meant to harvest, calculate, and circulate GNSS raw measurements, Google not only facilitated but encouraged industry and government to experiment with what otherwise seemed like innocuous, dormant calculations that every smartphone on the planet had been silently producing in the background since the early 2010s. This was no mistake on Google's part. Around 2010, the EGNSS Agency published a market report predictions that separated "core" GNSS raw measurement-enabled devices (non-smartphone devices) value against "enabled" GNSS raw measurement-enabled devices (smartphones). The former's projected market value was €58 billion at the time, the latter at more than double the former: €133 billion. Nearly a decade later, the EGNSSA projects that "consumer solutions" are expected to account for nearly half of a €2,525 trillion industry – with "data revenue of smartphones and tablets using location-based services" being the primary driver of the projected capital growth (European Global Navigation Satellite Systems Agency, 2019). Along the way, neighboring markets with seemingly unrelated connections to smartphones – such as rail, emergency response, spacecraft, critical infrastructure, maritime navigation, drones, and geomatics – are increasingly turning to research and development on GNSS raw measurements in ways that turn to the smartphone as a basis for testing.

Second, as Surveillance Studies scholars have argued for decades, with capital opportunity comes *function creep*: the transformative change in a data processing system's proper activity that causes a qualitative shift in functionality, resulting in the often high-risk redeployment, re-usage or repurposing of the system for unrelated uses (Koops, 2020). Technological change for-the-sake-of-change, particularly when it is "insufficiently acknowledged as transformative" within the context of capital accumulation and growth, tends to unfold without public consultation and debate, which establishes a dangerous precedent for potential civil rights and liberties harms. It is significant but not surprising that discussion of GNSS raw measurements (let alone five-year developments of PPP on smartphones), despite having been a focal point of intellectual curiosity and industrial development for years, is only now being discussed as a location privacy concern. Alas, this is precisely what is implied by the notion of function creep itself, in that technology being used for increasingly unrelated and risky purposes tends to happen well away from the purview of informed critique. By opening the door to GNSS raw measurements, smartphone users do not merely stand to have an improvement to the ability for the device to find itself in physical space with greater accuracy. These developments are catalyzed by the mutual coalescing of interest (Haggerty and Ericsson, 2003) in real-time, high-resolution tracking for security, surveillance, entertainment, and profit purposes. Moreover, what smartphone users stand to *lose* is the spatial ambiguity that otherwise mediates the extent to which they can be located in space and time.

Third, and most importantly, GNSS raw measurement collection by industry and government is a dangerously under-discussed imposition upon not only the ability for smartphone users to control the extent and circumstances that smartphone location services depend upon, it is also an unbridled imposition upon how the public, the media, and ourselves as critical thinkers imagine the very concept of "location privacy." Even if we can momentarily accept a modest definition of location privacy to mean the ability to be free from observation within a geophysical space, we must also immediately contend with the matter of how this is achievable in public space. To be private in public is to fashion the corporeal body with hats, sunglasses, and clothing that mediates gaze. To be private in public is to be protected by constitution, law, and civil rights that establish limits upon physical, emotional, and cognitive interaction between one another. To be private in public is also to have a sense of control of what digital measurements can and cannot be made about one's self, but that type of privacy depends upon fleeting senses of consent, proportionality, and third-party access permissions to asymmetrical data flows in our smartphones – especially those that users cannot easily negotiate or see. To further complicate the matter, Mahmoudi et al. (2020) remind us that urban space is latent with structural and systemic inequalities more often than not catalyzed by development motivated by the capital pursuit of data on our smartphones. These complications emerge during an important time where smartphone users are socialized into their location as well, or what Wilson (2012) calls *conspicuous mobility*: the making known in a way that clearly stands out and is obviously visible of one's location. "All too often," Shelton (2017) reminds us, "questions of how to conceive space and spatiality are pushed into the background." Perhaps as an intellectual consequence of both popular and even scholarly (Soja, 1980) tendencies to utilize Cartesian understandings of space as "physical and absolute" (Shelton, 2017), the conceptual preoccupation with imagining buildings, intersections, and sidewalks as concretely defined ontologically renders them as independent and nonnegotiable physical phenomena. People and their devices, however, are mobile and they are liquid. How they are represented has considerably more representational flexibility. But the processes that govern their representation are engineered, just like physical buildings. Location awareness is normalized through "check-ins" on social media platforms or on our devices themselves; there is a correlating tendency for technology to instantiate "a shift in the nature and scale of privacy as a social relation" (Elwood and Leszczynski, 2011). Manufacturers, content and service providers, and social media companies render citizens visible to themselves and one another with increasingly high-resolution representations of a person's geophysical surroundings. The actors facilitating this socialization are thus inevitably engaged in negotiating and (re)presenting the meaning, constitution, and boundaries of location privacy itself – but in processes that occur *beyond* the subject (Elwood and Leszczynski, 2011). For smartphone users, the notion of location privacy has more to do with Terms of Use Agreements and location services permission systems than it has to do with the actual, real-time spatial area within which citizen consumers can be rendered (un)knowable, (un)seeable, and (un)trackable. Accordingly, industrial and governmental access to smartphone GNSS raw measurements and their subsequent usage in funding competition sandboxes where engineers experiment within preexisting automated modeling, detection, and tracking systems is quintessential to the future of smartphone location privacy; to know, see, and track a user and their device within a 10-meter radius versus a sub-meter radius is the difference between *certainty* and *ambiguity*.

As Acquisti and Grossklags argue (2005), "incomplete information is relevant to privacy," particularly in the sense that controlling the amount of incomplete information that others can access about you dictates the integrity of one's own personal sphere. While E911 and apps such as What3Words remain squarely situated within emergency services discourses that will always have a stake in needing to accurately locate a device to potentially save a life, what does it means to be able to know or claim that a citizen can be located within a space smaller than a section of a sidewalk? Consider, for example, the usage of "geofencing" techniques used to monitor known and suspected infected citizens throughout the COVID-19 pandemic. The governments of Paraguay, the US, Australia, Indonesia, Switzerland, Italy, Vietnam, Qatar, Taiwan, and Saudi Arabia use software to virtually demarcate the boundaries of a citizen's home. Geofencing establishes a digital warning system: if a device leaves the fenced-in zone, the app can notify the police who, in the case of Taiwan, are then sent to immediately find the individual in question. Some may argue that there is considerable civic merit in being able to precisely track the device of an infected citizen for public safety purposes. However, in Indonesia, Switzerland, Vietnam, Qatar, Saudi Arabia, and the US, geofencing services are established in partnership with private telecommunication providers and private sector entrepreneurs, as evidenced by the Canadian firm Shopify's involvement in the creation of Canada's contact tracing app COVID Shield. What are the social implications of increasingly precise and decreasingly ambiguous location and movement data when they are introduced and become inextricably fused into the highly asymmetric lifeblood of pandemic era surveillance capitalism? What does it mean to user privacy when private companies play a role in curating and circulating location data that undermines the ability for a citizen to be ambiguous versus precisely known in terms of the direction they are travelling, the speed at which they move, and when they pause while traversing public spaces? These questions are not merely rhetorical. GNSS raw measurements were building blocks in the production of latitude and longitude coordinates sold to the US Department of Homeland Security by Predicio – a Paris-based mobile location analytics company – to enable the tracking of ten million Muslim Americans during the pandemic (Cox, 2021). The spaces within which these citizens were "known to exist" were Mosques – physical structures that are larger than the human body. Accordingly, what is at stake in collapsing physical spaces around the device via interventions such as PPP is the potential inability for citizens to be rendered ambiguous within spaces that prevailing societal norms otherwise establish as privacy-preserving; homes, mosques, apartments, grocery stores, and even public buildings ought to be recognized as geophysical buffers to location tracking, ones that are at risk of dissolving in the industrial wake of predictive smartphone location (over)engineering.

The industrial uptake of GNSS raw measurements is also being used in another way that will have dramatic consequences for smartphone location privacy: their usage to destroy *location spoofing*, the act of deceiving a GNSS receiver or tracking device by producing and/or transmitting incorrect location data. Location spoofing has a long and tumultuous history within the global GNSS community. In the mid to late 2000s, industry-driven concerns with fake location production situated such processes within the context of intentional counterfeiting and faking as an extension of malicious behavior (Hein et al., 2007; Nielsen et al., 2010). Whether within a handheld receiver or an official listening apparatus operated by airports or maritime regulation and security agencies, untrustworthy hackers and criminals seeking to mislead others by producing falsified location data has been quickly categorized as acts of, for example, international conflict (Humphreys et al., 2009). In 2019, the *Scientific American* reported on approximately 50 documented attempts of GPS jamming and interference at Manila's Ninoy Aquino International Airport where airliners' navigation system was targeted during take-off and landing approaches (Tullis, 2019). Reports of the like stirred up speculation regarding government navigation and defense system vulnerabilities worldwide, concerns that were further compounded by an increase in a correlating of global media interest around the Russian government's intentional injection of misleading location data into civilian receivers and maritime ships in an attempt to prevent foreign governments from using drones to track Vladimir Putin during his international travels (De Luce, 2019) – techniques that the Russian government had been testing and engineering for some time (Hambling, 2017).

And yet the discourse on location faking leaves little argumentative or conceptual space to account for spoofing in the name of location privacy. One of the most significant social consequences of technology manufacturers fighting against smartphone users was the near-immediate disappearance of privacy-driven applications called "tweaks": highly customized smartphone applications that are unauthorized for distribution in an official application marketplace (Cooke, 2020). There is a longstanding yet largely understudied legacy of tweaks available for iPhone users, which are made available through a process called jailbreaking, which Apple works hard to prevent. Jailbreaking allows users to modify or install unapproved software, such as tweaks. While Apple has long since the beginning of the jailbreaking movement maintained that it not only violates their policy but makes devices insecure, researchers at the University of California, Santa Barbara, revealed through a study of 526 tweaks and 825 iOS apps that they are in fact safer, leaked less data than corporately developed apps, and are less intrusive upon user privacy and security than tweaks (Greenberg, 2012). Among this community of unauthorized tweaks are ones specifically designed to alter iOS behavior to provide privacy protections that exposed and fundamentally altered how iPhone devices handle location data. For example, BegoneCIA and locdown allow users to completely disable location services. Others like GPS Master, GPS Cheat, and Location Faker provide an extra step of *spoofing* the device's location and travel history in ways that affect the location data receiving and processing behavior of apps like Google Maps, YouTube, Twitter, and so on.

The primary imposition of GNSS raw measurements upon location spoofing is that they may prevent it from happening altogether. In the past five years, multiple geoscience and app development publications demonstrate new methods for using GNSS raw measurements to forensically analyze embedded carrier-to-noise ratio and automatic gain control data variables produced by the phone's chipset. By analyzing these specific GNSS raw measurement variables, these methods compare and contrast location data produced by apps, such as privacy-preserving tweaks. Because the method pulls highly sensitive raw measurement data directly from the receiver and thus satellite signal streams, they are treated as a source of location truth – one that is used to declare that a given app is lying about where "it is," geophysically speaking (Lee et al., 2019). For example, a corporation-friendly Android app called GNS-SAlarm is designed to "combat the threat presented by malicious spoofing" (Miralles et al., 2018). This app builds upon the previous method by combining GNSS variables with inertial sensor data and additional pseudorange metrics found in the GNSS raw measurement stream to assist industry partners to detect whether or not a user is faking their own location on their own device when using their services. Despite corporate discourse maintaining that spoofing is a threat, it also needs to be thought about in the context of *preserving location privacy.* Apps like Grindr aggressively track and share user location widely, making some vulnerable communities that Grindr serves increasingly more insecure as they travel while using the app (Latimer, 2018). Moreover, walk-through blog posts and virtual private network (VPN) marketing campaigns (Marks, 2021) in support of the need for smartphone location privacy counter corporate anti-spoofing discourse by promoting the need for spoofing; simulating one's whereabouts prevents unsolicited advertising, stalking, profiling, and as such can play a fundamentally important role in preventing political and religious discrimination. There is indeed a tension here between GNSS raw measurements with how smartphone users come to expect and understand their own control over their devices. While the industrial and governmental uptake of

GNSS raw measurements may be promoted to enhance the experience of the smartphone user, the developments that these data are used in are increasingly decentralized; this is particularly problematic in a context where these data are being used forensically to judge and co-opt user location honestly – a development that further emphasizes the need for scholars to think more critically about the future of smartphone location privacy in the face of data extraction and calculation processes that take well below and beyond "GPS coordinates."

References

Acquisti, Andy and Grossklags, Jens. 2005. "Privacy and Rationality in Individual Decision Making". *IEEE Security and Privacy Magazine* 3(1), pp. 26–33.

Adekunle, Isioye Olalekan. 2014. "As assessment of Ionospheric Error Mitigation Techniques for GNSS Estimation in the Low Equatorial African Region". *Positioning* 5(1), pp. 27–35.

Andrianarison, Maheziro, Mohamed Sahmoudi, and Rene Jr. Landry. 2018. "New Strategy of Collaborative Acquisition for Connected GNSS Receivers in Deep Urban Environments". *Positioning* 9(3), pp. 23–46.

Bisnath, Sunil, John Aggrey, Garrett Seespread, and Marinder Gill. 2018. "Innovation: Examining Precise Point Positioning Now and in the Future", 19 March. *GPS World Magazine*. Available: https://www.gpsworld.com/innovation-examining-precise-point-positioning-now-and-in-the-future/

Brandi, Paolo. 2019. "Android API Level, Backward and Forward Compatibility". 9 June. *AndroidPub*. Available: https://medium.com/android-news/android-api-level-backward-and-forward-compatibility-10e6d31cb848

Cooke, Thomas N. 2020. "Metadata, Jailbreaking, and the Cybernetic Governmentality of iOS: Or, the Need to Distinguish Digital Privacy from Digital Privacy". *Surveillance & Society* 18(1), pp. 91–103.

Cox, Joseph. 2021. "Google Kicks Location Data Broker That Sold Muslim Prayer App User Data". 9 February. *VICE News*. Available: https://www.vice.com/en/article/dy8eba/google-predicio-ban-muslim-prayer-app

Crichton, Danny and Arman Tabatabai. 2018. "The GPS Wars Have Begun". 21 December. *TechCrunch*. Available: https://techcrunch.com/2018/12/21/the-gps-wars-have-begun/

De Luce, Dan. 2019. "Russia 'Spoofing' GPS on Vast Scale to Stop Drones from Approaching Putin, Report Says". 26 March. *NBC News*. Available: https://www.nbcnews.com/news/vladimir-putin/russia-spoofing-gps-vast-scale-stop-drones-approaching-putin-report-n987376Elwood, Sarah and Leszczynski, Agnieszka. 2011. "Privacy, reconsidered: New Representations, Data Practices, and the Geoweb". *Geoforum* 42(1), pp. 6–15.

European Global Navigation Satellite Systems Agency. 2017. "Using Raw GNSS Measurements on Android Devices: White Paper". EGNSSA GNSS Raw Measurements Task Force.

European Global Navigation Satellite Systems Agency. 2019. "GNSS Market Report. Issue 6". Available: https://www.euspa.europa.eu/system/files/reports/market_report_issue_6_v2.pdf

Greenberg, Andy. 2012. "Unauthorized iPone and iPad Apps Leak Private Data Less Often than Approved Ones". *Forbes Magazine* 14 February 2012. Available: https://www.forbes.com/sites/andygreenberg/2012/02/14/unauthorized-iphone-and-ipad-apps-leak-private-data-less-often-than-approved-ones/?sh=2dc45c0b187f

Google Analytics Help. 2021. https://support.google.com/analytics/answer/7686480?hl=en

Haggerty, Kevin D. and Richard V. Ericsson. 2003. "The Surveillant Assemblage". *The British Journal of Sociology* 51(4), pp. 605–622.

Hambling, David. 2017. "Ships Fooled in GPS Spoofing Attack Suggest Russian Cyberweapon". 10 August. *NewScientist*. Available: https://www.newscientist.com/article/2143499-ships-fooled-in-gps-spoofing-attack-suggest-russian-cyberweapon/

Hein, Gunter W., Rodriguez, Jose Angel Avila, Wallner, Stefan, Eissfeller, Bernd, Pany, Thomas, and Hartl, Philipp. 2007. "Envisioning a Future GNSS System of Systems". *Inside GNSS Magazine* January/February 2007. Available: https://www.insidegnss.com/auto/Jan%20Feb%2007-Working Papers.pdf

Humphreys, Todd E., Ledvina, Brent M., Psiaki, Mark L., O'Hanlon, Brady, and Kintner Jr., P. M. 2008. Assessing the Spoofing Threat: Development of a Portable GPS Civilian Spoofer. In *Proceedings of ION GNSS Conference.* ION, Savanna, GA: 2314–2325.

Koops, Bert-Jaap. 2020. "The Concept of Function Creep". *Law, Innovation and Technology* 1. Available: https://papers.ssrn.com/sol3/papers.cfm?abstract_id=3547903

Lake, Robert. 2017. "Big Data, Urbgan Governance, and the Ontological Politics of hyperindividualism". *Big Data & Society* 4(1), pp. 1–10.

Lamontagne, Guillaume, Rene Jr. Landry, and Ammar B. Kouki. 2012. "Direct RF Sampling GNSS Receiver Design and Jitter Analysis". *Positioning* 3(4), pp. 46–61.

Latimer, Brian. 2018. "Grindr security flaw exposes users' location data", *NBC News Tech & Media* 18 March 2018. Available: https://www.nbcnews.com/feature/nbc-out/security-flaws-gay-dating-app-grindr-expose-users-location-data-n858446

Lee, Dong-Kyeong, Mattias Petit, Damian Miralles, Sherman Lo, and Dennis Akos. 2019. "Analysis of Raw GNSS Measurements Derived Navigation Solutions from Mobile Sources with Inertial Sensors". Proceedings from the 32nd International Technical Meeting of the Satellite Division of the Institute of Navigation (ION GNSS+ 2019). Available: https://www.ion.org/publications/abstract.cfm?articleID=17070

Lei, Zhuo, Li, Min, Li, Wenwen, and Jiang, Kacai. 2021. "Performance Evaluation of Single-Frequency Precise Point Positioning and Its Use in the Android Smartphone". *Remote Sensing* 13(23), pp. 4894–4913.

Lohan, Elena Simona. 2011. "Limited Bandwidths and Correlation Ambiguities: Do They Co-Exist in Galileo Receivers". *Positioning* 2(1), pp. 14–21.

Lopatto, Elizabeth. 2020. "Even Google Engineers are Confused about Google's Privacy Settings". 26 August. The Verge News. Available: https://www.theverge.com/2020/8/26/21403202/google-engineers-privacy-settings-lawsuit-arizona-doubleclick

Ma, Lin, Yanyun Sun, Yuqi Zhang, Bing Han, Yi Wang, and Lin Li. 2019. "GNSS/MET Station Equipment Maintenance and Product Application". *Journal of Geoscience and Environmental Protection* 7, pp. 105–113.

Mahmoudi, Dillon, Lubitow, Amy, and Christensen, MacKenzie A. 2020. "Reproducing Spatial Inequality: The Sustainability Fix and Barriers to Urban Mobility in Portland, Oregon". *Urban Geography* 41(6), pp. 801–822.

Malkos, Steve. 2016. "Making Android Sensors and Location Work for You". *Presentation at the Annual Conference of Google I/O 2016.* 19 May 2016. Available: https://www.youtube.com/watch?v=OEvycEMoLUg

Marks, Tove. 2021. "Staying Safe on Grindr: How To Protect Your Privacy". *VPNOverview.* 11 March. Available: https://vpnoverview.com/privacy/apps/privacy-grindr/

McKinnis, Micah. 2013. "Russian "Spy Stations": A Clear and Present Danger?" 16 December. *The Daily Signal.* Available: https://www.dailysignal.com/2013/12/16/russian-spy-stations-clear-present-danger/

Miralles, Damian, Nathan Levigne, Dennis M. Akos, Juan Blanch, and Sherman Lo. 2018. "Android Raw GNSS Measurements as a New Anti-Spoofing and Anti-Jamming Solution". Proceedings from the 31st International Technical Meeting of the Satellite Division of the Institute of Navigation (ION GNSS+ 2018). Available: https://www.ion.org/publications/abstract.cfm?articleID=15883

Mollaiyan, Kaveh, Rock Santerre, Rene Jr. Landry. 2013. "Acquisition of Weak Signals in Multi-Constellation Frequency Domain Receivers". *Positioning* 4, pp. 144–152.

Nakashima, Ryan. 2018. "AP Exclusive: Google tracks your movements, like it or not". 13 August. The Associated Press. Available: https://apnews.com/article/north-america-science-technology-business-ap-top-news-828aefab64d4411bac257a07c1af0ecb

Nielsen, John, Ali Broumandan, and Gerard Lachapelle. 2010. "Spoofing Detection with a Moving Handheld Receiver". 1 September. *GPS World Magazine.* Available: https://www.gpsworld.com/gnss-systemreceiver-designspoofing-detection-and-mitigation-10456/

Pace, Scott, Gerald P. Frost, Irving Lachow, David R. Frelinger, Donna Fossum, Don Wassem, and Monica M. Pinto. 1995. *The Global Positioning System: Assessing National Policies.* Santa Monica, CA: RAND Corporation.

Personal Information Protection and Electronics Documents Act (2005) June 23. 2015. https://laws-lois.justice.gc.ca/eng/acts/P-8.6/index.html

Sarkola, Pekka. 2000. "Location Services for Mobile Phone Users". Proceedings from the 3rd AGILE Conference on Geographic Information

Science, 25–27 May. Available: http://citeseerx.ist.psu.edu/viewdoc/download?doi=10.1.1.455.4817&rep=rep1&type=pdf

Schmidt, M.S. and Schmitt, E. 2013. "A Russian GPS Using U.S. Soil Stirs Spy Fears". *New York Times*, Nov 16 2013. Available: https://www.nytimes.com/2013/11/17/world/europe/a-russian-gps-using-us-soil-stirs-spy-fears.html

Shelton, Taylor. 2017. "Spatialities of Data: Mapping Social Media 'Beyond the Geotag'". *GeoJournal* 82, pp. 721–734.

Soja, Edward W. 1980. "The Socio-Spatial Dialectic". *Annals of the Association of American Geographers* 780(2), pp. 207–225.

Taoufiq, Jouan, Bouziani Mourad, Azzouzi Rachid, and Christine Amory-Mazaudier. 2018. "Study of Ionospheric Variability Using GNSS Observations". *Positioning* 9(4), pp. 79–96.

TASS Russian News Agency. "Rogozin instructs to investigate GPS operation in Russia". 25 November 2013. TASS Russian News Agency. Available: https://tass.com/russia/709005

Tullis, Paul. 2019. "GPS Is Easy To Hack, and the U.S. Has No Backup". 1 December. *The Scientific American*. Available: https://www.scientificamerican.com/article/gps-is-easy-to-hack-and-the-u-s-has-no-backup/

Tynan, Dan. 2010. "Why Location Privacy is Important". 25 June. *ComputerWorld*. Available: https://www.computerworld.com/article/2752981/why-location-privacy-is-important.html

Van Diggelen, and Frank Stephen Tromp. 2009. *A-GPS: Assisted GPS, GNSS, and SBAS*. Boston: Artech House.

Wilson, Matthew W. 2012. "Location-based Services, Conspicuous Mobility, and the Location-aware Future". *Geoforum* 43, pp. 1266–1275.

Wilson, Richard. 2011. "Qualcomm Adds GLONASS Positioning to Smartphones". 30 May. *ElectronicsWeekly*. Available: https://www.electronicsweekly.com/news/design/communications/qualcomm-adds-glonass-positoning-to-smartphones-2011-05/

Note

1 This chapter reflects ongoing research into location processing in Android smartphones. This work is supported by "A Day in the Life of Metadata," a large multidisciplinary collaboration between social scientists and computer engineers to reverse-engineer and critically investigate how third-party companies and governments access and ascribe meaning to hidden location data within Google devices. For further information, visit aditlom.org.

Index